"The Potato Chip Difference *clearly presents the highly useful application of sound marketing strategy to the job search process, enabling job seekers to better position and differentiate themselves. Because of its clear strategic guidance, the book is particularly useful in the early stages of a job search.*"

T. W. O'Neal
Senior Vice President, IMG

* * * * *

"*In the executive search business we see the wisdom of Goodman's advice almost daily. We work exclusively with marketing people. These are senior-level executives who wouldn't dream of creating a marketing _plan_ without first developing a well-conceived marketing strategy. Yet when it comes to their own professional career too often they seem to ignore career strategy in pursuit of off-target short-term "opportunities." The result of this oversight is an unfocused career path with too many unexplainable job changes.*"

John Bissell, Managing Partner
Gundersen Partners, L.L.C.

* * * * *

"*Goodman's* The Potato Chip Difference *is a valuable tool for anyone thinking about or looking for a new job. His unique contribution (as a marketing consultant) is guidance through the self-positioning process: How to recognize, evaluate, and organize your talents so as to highlight them in the mind of an employer ... and to get the job you deserve!*"

Akasha Ames, President
The Snowdon Group

"The Potato Chip Difference *is an informative and easy to read guide that offers lots of good suggestions and tools that you will want to spend time absorbing and using. I recommend this book because it focuses on the planning phase of the self-marketing effort — when you determine the strategy that will guide everything else you do. This is often the most neglected phase of the job search process because so many of us want to jumpstart our searches by pushing resumes out the door so that the phone starts to ring. Take time to make a difference in your search. Read this book and put it to use. It will make a difference for you."*

Ellen Stuhlmann, Managing Director
ExecuNet's Executive Insider Newsletter

* * * * *

"The Potato Chip Difference *is for you if you want to spend some time learning new tools to better understand yourself, as well as better prepare you to find — and land — that ideal job with the ideal employer. ... The job search is all about using marketing skills to better position, present, and sell yourself to potential employers — and this book will make you better prepared for your next job search."*

Dr. Randall S. Hansen, Ph.D.
QuintessentialCareers.com

* * * * *

"With all the 'help' out there for job seekers — books, websites, career coaches, you name it — most people need a good road map. The Potato Chip Difference *is an excellent 'first read' for a job seeker."*

Matthew Sitelman, Senior Vice President
6 Figure Jobs (www.6figurejobs.com)

THE
POTATO CHIP
DIFFERENCE

THE
POTATO CHIP
DIFFERENCE

**How to apply leading edge
marketing strategies to
landing the job you want**

Michael A. Goodman

Dialogue
Press
Westport, Connecticut

Dialogue
Press
P.O. Box 657
Westport, CT 06881-0657

Publisher's Cataloguing-in-Publication
(Provided by Quality Books, Inc.)

Goodman, Michael A.
    The potato chip difference: how to apply leading edge
marketing strategies to landing the job you want / Michael A.
Goodman. -- 1st ed.
    p. cm.
    Includes bibliographical references.
    LCCN: 00-104975
    ISBN: 0-9702088-0-4

    1. Career development. 2. Job hunting. 3. Career changes.
4. Vocational guidance. 5. Marketing.   I. Title

HF5382.7.G66 2000   650.14
                                        QBI00-500094

Contents

Acknowledgments

Certainly, writing this book gave me an opportunity to utilize my own skill set and experience to make a positive difference for people who find themselves in the job market. I couldn't have done it alone, though, and I want to acknowledge the people whose assistance and support made the final product possible.

Thanks first to Jenny Bevins for a great job of editing and proofreading. The readability of this book has been substantially improved as a result of her diligence. Thanks too to Barry Tarshis and Dick Seclow for their encouragement, comments, and insights into both the substance of this book and the whole world of book publishing, which until now was totally foreign to me.

There were lots of others who knowingly and unknowingly had a hand in this book. Rich Gold, my consulting partner for the last twenty years, has a very strong strategic focus. I know I've learned a lot from him, and much of what I've learned has found its way onto these pages. Phil DeCocco, a world-class human resources expert with whom I had the privilege of working at Playtex back in the late '70s, was probably my first real mentor on the subject of career planning, selection interviewing and people development. He'll recognize his own words and thoughts at several places in this book.

And numerous clients and former clients have made a real impact on my understanding of key elements in this book. They not only provided feedback and support as I honed my own skills in bringing strategic planning and marketing expertise to bear on their companies' issues, but they taught me a lot about management and people sensitivity through their own actions and examples.

Finally, the people I've counseled over the years have made a contribution too. I've taken a few examples from their lives to illustrate points in this book, always protecting their privacy and identity of course. They've actually taught me as much as I've taught them, I'm sure, though I know it wasn't their intent at the time.

And a special kind of gratitude is due my wife Connie and sons Jason and Brian, all of whom provided encouragement and support as I worked on this project. Jason even proofread an early draft as he began his own job search, and Brian asked me to review his resume and job-search plans at about the midpoint.

I can only hope now that this book accomplishes its mission — landing YOU the job you really want.

Michael A. Goodman
Westport, Connecticut

Preface

Changing jobs is becoming more common and more challenging every year. At any given point in time, there are more than 23 million Americans actively considering or looking for a new job. Moreover, that number is increasing each year as the job pool expands, new companies are established at an unprecedented rate, new technology creates jobs and opportunities that didn't even exist a year earlier, home-based businesses and self-employment become an attractive alternative for many, and the culture accepts frequent moves as an expected and normal part of good career progress and self-fulfillment.

Consider that more than twenty-seven percent of workers have been with their current employer less than one year, and the average American worker's tenure with an employer is only about forty-two months. That number is decreasing every year, and if the current trend continues, the average will be less than three years before 2005 is over.

This phenomenon is posing a real problem for job seekers not only because it means that there is more competition in the job market, but also because the model we've all been using for career planning was developed in an earlier era, when it was not at all uncommon for workers to spend their entire careers at one company — or two at most. As a result, the job search process and career planning in general were not subject to frequent and regular exploration and redefinition. You did it once or twice, and then you simply focused on doing your job and getting promoted.

As a professional marketing and management consultant, this strikes me as a product life cycle problem — in reverse order. What used to behave like a mature market — with high brand (or company) loyalty — has become instead like a new market in the rapid growth phase. During rapid growth, a product category experiences significant new trial, brand switching, and a high consumer need for current information.

In fact, the basic principles of good marketing strategy — including an understanding of product life-cycles — can provide an excellent framework for addressing career planning and job switching in this new environment. Having spent my entire career in marketing management, this should have been obvious to me from the outset. In practice, it wasn't.

For years, people have come to me for career advice. That's probably because I've worked and consulted for some very large and well-respected companies: I have had an opportunity to understand their corporate cultures, gain the confidence and trust of senior management, and have substantial input — with responsibility for recruiting, hiring, training, and evaluating new staff members. The advice seekers were essentially networking and asking me whether I knew of a position that might be right for them.

Then at some point it occurred to me that these people — the job seekers — were faced with having to market themselves, and they were having a problem understanding the parallels between marketing a product, service, or company and marketing themselves to their next employer. They were oblivious to the direct and immediate value of developing and implementing a sound marketing strategy for themselves.

That's when I began to think more seriously about those parallels and study the process by which people make career decisions, change employers, seek new jobs, and pursue their personal objectives in the workplace. It was a fascinating journey, and it resulted in this book — *The Potato Chip Difference: How to apply leading edge marketing strategies to landing the job you want.*

This book will take you step by step through the strategy development process — the same process that leading management consulting firms use with their large corporate clients — and will show you how to apply the basic principles of good marketing to the most important product in your life — YOU.

If you will take the time and make the effort to understand the steps involved in strategy development, you'll end up with a better plan, in a shorter time, and with a more satisfying outcome than if you simply start sending out resumes, calling headhunters and answering employment ads.

This book will show you how. The perspective and approach I'll explain in the pages that follow have already been proven in the real world of product and service marketing, and they've helped a number of personal acquaintances and career planners set their own job search strategies. I'm convinced they can work for anyone. Of course, you may want to read other books and get other points of view. You owe it to yourself to begin with the broadest perspective possible. I even suggest some of the references I like best in the course of the discussion ahead. The important thing is that you start with a sound strategic approach — and that's what this book is all about.

Let's get started. Strategy first.

Chapter 1

The Objective Is To Get the Job

I'm a big believer in stating your objectives right up front and in plain, straightforward language. So let's begin by agreeing that the reason you're reading this book, and the reason I wrote it, is to get you the job you want. Every sentence you're about to read was written beneath a big sign reading "The Objective is to Get the Job."

Of course, I'm not talking about just any job. I'm talking about the job that is tailor-made for you — your ideal job. And it's out there waiting for you. The challenge is to find it and convince the employer that you're also the perfect match for his needs — a win/win situation, if ever there was one.

In consulting (and in business), this would qualify as a classical marketing project. And perhaps this is the right place to share a bias and dispel any negative preconceived notions you may have about marketing and marketing strategy. After all, what we're really doing here is marketing a product — YOU!

Do I really have to *market* myself?

By "marketing," I don't mean hyping, exaggerating, or selling someone something they didn't know they needed. That's a really unfortunate image the discipline has picked up over the years. It's also important to distinguish between sales and marketing. I've heard "selling" defined as pushing what you have to your customers. That's a bit limiting and disparaging, but it does capture the essential role of sales. (A kinder and more appropriate definition of sales might be "management of the customer interface.") Marketing, by way of contrast, is figuring out what customers are going to need and finding a way to get it to them on terms that are satisfactory to both of you.

Notice that the primary focus in marketing is on customers' future needs. These needs might not even be evident to the customer today. A good marketer can look in the rearview mirror and, with a little experience, figure out what the road ahead is going to look like. Of course, the customer is usually too close to today's problems to really analyze what's happening and project future requirements.

Once the future needs are identified, we're going to have to figure out how to deliver a solution on terms that we can both live with.

Let me give you a real-life example. Many years ago, before HMOs and other health care management options became commonplace, I had occasion to work on a project for a hospital management company. Their revenues were slipping because of a trend toward shorter hospital stays and increased use of outpatient services. They wanted to look for ways to capture a greater share of the market in order to regain lost revenues, and they called in the "marketing experts" because they thought the problem might be solved by advertising or promoting their product with doctors or patients in a more effective way.

By the time we finished the project, my client was in the insurance business, offering a very attractive major medical plan to local employers and waiving deductibles and copayments when patients used their hospitals and medical staff.

That solution to the client's business problem was a direct result of good marketing strategy. It anticipated a future need for affordable health care. It also shifted the customer focus from doctors and patients, who had little incentive to control costs, to employers, who were ultimately footing the bill and thus stood to realize a significant savings. And the client's solution included a way to deliver its product and service on terms that were beneficial to both the various customer constituencies and themselves.

Sales, in this example, was the function charged with presenting the concept to the target audience (local employers) and managing the relationship between the hospital/insurance company and the customers. Sales was charged with taking the orders for what marketing had developed.

In a very real sense, the sales function is part of marketing. It's the part charged with managing the interface and relationship with direct customers.

For your job search, you're going to need to assume the role of head marketing strategist first. Later, after the strategies and plans are developed, you'll shift gears and become the sales department. We'll discuss all of this in the coming chapters. For now, let's be sure we have the strategy right.

Developing the strategy that will get the job

To begin the process, your first sub-objective is to figure out what your ideal employer is going to be looking for and showing up with it in a way so that he or she can't possibly say no.

There are a lot of books on library and bookstore shelves that deal with resume writing, career planning, and various elements of the interviewing and job selection process. Some of them are even very good. The problem is you'd have to spend hours, or even days and months, to go through them all and figure out which ones are going to be most useful to you. And then you'd have a lot of "pieces" with no "whole." You'd be missing the big idea or overall game plan.

This book is going to short-circuit all of that and tell you exactly what you need to know about developing the *strategy* that will get you your next job. I'll recommend a few other books you may want to read as part of the process, but the focus will be on guiding you through the critically important steps in developing a winning strategy for one of the most important projects of your life.

Finding a job is obviously a weighty subject with broad appeal. Finding the "next job" (and presumably one that's better than the one you have, or had most recently) is a topic that will be relevant and important to just about every one of us at one time or another in the coming years. Americans are changing jobs, companies, and careers more frequently now than at any time in our history, and there's nothing on the horizon that suggests this is going to change anytime soon.

There are a number of reasons for this phenomenon, but there's no need to become academic about social trends when the real objective of this book is to provide immediate, proscriptive help for people who find themselves in the job market. It's generally not a time when theory and macroeconomics seem very relevant.

It is important though to recognize the job search process for what it is — a very serious marketing job, with a unique product: You!

As a professional marketing and management consultant for the last twenty years, I've seen the entire range of marketing strategies, for all sorts of products and services, and they run the gamut from "knock-your-socks-off great" to "embarrassingly bad." I've probably seen just as many job seekers, and the range of quality in their strategies extends across the same scale. I've also been in a position to hire, fire, interview, recruit, evaluate, and make recommendations about job applicants across a wide range of industries and company types, and I've read dozens of books about all aspects of both the recruiting and job-seeking processes.

That's why this book now exists. You could spend the better part of a year (or even more) reading up on the subject, refining your own strategies and testing various approaches. But I'm guessing you don't have that kind of time or patience. You want a job — NOW.

If you'll track through this book, take the "homework" assignments seriously and invest just a little time and money reading and researching the few subjects noted, you'll have all you really need. Of course, you're welcome to do more, but I seriously question whether it will provide sufficient incremental benefit to justify the added time and expense — not to mention the stress factor.

How did I get here?

There are four different sets of circumstances that put people out of work and into heavy-duty job-seeking mode: downsizing, firing, retiring and just moving on. A brief word about each is probably in order.

♦ **Downsizing** is a generic term for "job elimination." It might be the result of a corporate merger, a change in strategic direction for the company, a massive reorganization, and so forth. The distinguishing factor is that it's not the employee being terminated (what an unfortunate phrase!), but the job itself being eliminated. It's like not having a chair to sit in when the music stops.

♦ **Firing**, by way of contrast, is specific to the employee. It may be cause related — poor performance, insubordination, and so on — or it may be a personality thing, in which the employee is not seen as fitting in. The buzz words are often "…it's not working out…"

♦ **Retiring**, on the surface, is fairly self-explanatory. Worth noting, though, is that more and more companies are changing the rules along the way, and offering too-good-to-resist early retirement packages. While these are often in everyone's best financial interests, they frequently put people out of work before they're mentally or emotionally prepared for retirement, and they join compatriots in the other categories, competing for a finite number of available jobs.

♦ Finally there's "**moving on**" — a phenomenon in which the employee decides that there's greener grass somewhere else and voluntarily enters (or reenters) the job market, changing employers or even career paths of his or her own volition.

Regardless of which of these phenomena have led you to this book, you'll soon discover you have a lot in common with people in the other "how I got here" categories. The emotions you will experience — fear, anticipation, excitement, happiness, sadness, anger — are pretty much the same, and the traditional approaches you will likely use to find the next stepping stone in your professional life are almost identical.

In the pages that follow, I'm going to suggest a course of action that is more likely to get you what you want, with less wasted energy and angst, faster and with greater certainty than the "traditional approaches." Of course, you can always hedge your bet, by going down multiple paths at the same time. I would submit though that there's not much to be gained by spinning your wheels this way, and you could increase your anxiety level to the point that you're actually subverting your real goal.

Finally, it's only fair that you understand my biases too. The last thirty years of my life have been devoted to marketing, general management, and strategic planning. As the old saying goes, "when you're a hammer, every problem looks like a nail." Accordingly, you'll find that I approach the job search process from a strategic point of view before I ever begin to develop or implement tactical plans. I also look at the prospective employee — that's you — as a "product" that needs to be "marketed" or presented honestly and in its best light. And it is my objective to help you view the product — yourself — in the same kind of objective way your next employer will.

One more caveat. Throughout this book, I'm going to be assuming that the job seeker is a manager, or management candidate, in a white-collar, professional environment. The basic principles apply to everyone, but I've chosen to keep it simple, be consistent, and use those kinds of positions as a "base case." Making the translation to a blue-collar situation, or academia, or a clerical job, shouldn't be very difficult.

Let's get into the strategic development process.

Chapter 2

The Strategic Development Process

The process for creating strategic marketing plans for a product or company has three very clearly defined steps: the situation analysis, positioning, and marketing strategy development. Since you're going to want to create your own strategic marketing plan — for YOU — it is important to understand exactly what's involved in each step, and how the whole thing flows and fits together.

The situation analysis

The **situation analysis** is arguably the most important component of the process because it provides the foundation for the other two and therefore the underpinning of the whole task. It's also the most time-consuming component — often extending over a period of three or four months in some businesses or industries.

Don't worry. Your own situation analysis doesn't need to take nearly that long, but it's important that you understand what the requirements are, because short-cutting or skipping part of it will ultimately undermine the foundation of your effort.

The objective of the situation analysis is to understand the product, the marketplace, and their relationship to one another in as thorough and objective a way as you can. The first requirement is thorough and accurate data gathering. The next is analyzing the data, which sometimes leads to still more data gathering and additional analysis. Then you'll want to assess the significance of what you've learned and determine how well the pieces fit together. We call this "assessing the product-market fit."

When working with a major client, I typically start the process by visiting the R&D center and talking with the product development team, process engineers, and quality control staff. I'm trying to learn what they think the product is, why and how it works, and what its problems, shortcomings, and future development needs are. After all, these are the product's "parents," so to speak, and they probably know it on a technical level better than anyone else.

Most of the time, despite the fact that I have an engineering degree, the client company's engineers, scientists, and Ph.D. chemists tell me things that are way over my head. I've been in laboratories dealing with advanced composite materials, electronic pre-press hardware and software, apparel design and manufacturing, biotechnology research, medical equipment, and some disciplines I'm not even sure I could categorize. Of course, I've also met with people whose products I understood a bit better — food preparation and nutrition experts, automobile repair professionals, and even men's and women's underwear designers. And there were some who were in the middle of that spectrum — insurance underwriters, for example, who work their own kind of magic developing products for the financial services industry.

In every case though I'm looking and listening for some iden-tification of the key issues, offering components and buzz words that are unique to the product and industry. I want to be at least as familiar with it as the customers are, because I'm going to be talk-ing to them next and I need to be able to make them comfortable that I'm not such a novice that they can dismiss me completely.

Once I have the product knowledge piece complete, I like to speak to the sales team. I want their perspective on the product and I also want to get their insights on the customer base. Often, I'll spend a few days actually making calls with a salesperson, just to observe the process and discover the unique decision-making ap-proach taken by people in the marketplace.

I also collect a stack of recent trade journals. I want to look at the ads to see who the players are, and I want to read what the thought-leaders are saying about what's going on in the industry. And if I can get my hands on any current market research that would give me additional understanding about the target audience (that's our term for customers usually), I want to analyze it and make sure I understand what it means.

This is all very important background work, and it's highly relevant to the process you're going to follow in setting your job search strategy, so let me spend a little more time describing one specific example of a good situation analysis.

An example from the farm

The client was a leading agricultural products manufacturer and the specific crop we were working on was corn. That meant I also had to understand a little about soybeans as well, because it's standard practice for farmers to rotate corn and soybeans every year, and last year's crop of each can affect this year's crop of the other in some important ways.

I grew up and lived my entire life in the city. I had only been on a farm once before in my life — for about six hours, twenty-five years earlier. I was clearly not in my comfort zone. I'd done my homework however, in the labs and with the sales force, and I figured I would just have to see what I could learn on a real working farm.

I spent three months in Nebraska, Iowa, Illinois, Indiana and Minnesota — meeting with farmers, feed and seed store owners, their other suppliers, grain elevator operators, and brokers. By the time I was finished I had learned about commodity trading, hog and cattle raising, agricultural lending, equipment sales, rural life, and a whole lot about the issues farmers face every day of their lives. I really felt as if I'd walked a few miles in their shoes.

It turned out in this case, as it does in most, that the situation analysis really paid off in a big way. I discovered that the bankers who financed the corn crop were every bit as important a target audience for my client as the farmers who actually bought the product, and the client had never even thought about lenders as being part of the real customer base. Needless to say, I had to go back to many of the farming communities to meet with bank lending officers once the initial analysis was complete.

What does it all mean?

When the data gathering is really finished — when you've learned almost everything you can about the product and marketplace — it's time to sift through all the notes and learnings and begin to assess the product-market fit. What are the customers going to need? Does the current offering fill that need, or is it lacking in some important way? Are there offering elements other than the product itself that could prove important? How does the product fit into the customers' lives? Are there important influences whose needs should be considered (like the bankers who finance the crop, for example)?

Addressing all of these questions and issues is part of the situation analysis phase. I think you can see why it's so important to do a thorough job of it.

Positioning

With the situation analysis in hand, it's time to determine what is unique about the product. How is it different from competitors, from other products in the client's own line, from previous versions or incarnations of the same product? In short, why should someone want it?

When we deal with this phase of your own strategic planning process, I'll go into more detail about the positioning process. For now, just understand that the objective is to articulate a clear and simple statement (called a "promise") that accurately defines the unique benefit that the target audience should expect when they buy your product or service. The statement should also offer a simple explanation of why the benefit promise should be believed (called a "reason why").

Actually, developing a good positioning statement is one of those things that gets easier when you do it more often. That's one of the reasons consultants who deal with positioning all the time are usually able to do a faster, better job than a client who only deals with positioning once every few years. I'm going to show you how to do it for yourself the first time, with all the precision and quality that an experienced pro could impart.

The reason positioning is so important — for a product, a company or YOU — is that once you understand the uniqueness of an offering, you can take full advantage of that uniqueness in every aspect of the marketing strategy.

Think about the unique positioning, for example, of Lay's potato chips. For years they were promoted as being "America's favorite potato chip — so good nobody can eat just one." From a positioning standpoint, what that means is Lay's outsells all other potato chips because people like the taste and crispness.

That positioning is truly unique because only one brand can be the largest selling brand, and the benefit to the target audience consumer is that the product will satisfy their craving for a salty snack chip better than any of the (lesser selling) alternatives.

You get the idea. We'll talk later about what makes some positioning statements better than others, and what the most important criteria are in developing and judging a positioning direction. In fact, you'll see why the potato chip analogy is perfect for your job search and career planning process.

In a typical project, I will spend anywhere from four to six weeks developing positioning, often testing, revising, and refining the original statement ten or twelve times before I'm satisfied with it. Because of its importance to the rest of the strategy, I don't want to compromise the result just to save a week or two on the client's timetable. You're going to want to devote a lot of time to your own positioning, but with a good foundation from your situation analysis, it shouldn't take you more than a couple of weeks.

Marketing strategy

In a typical strategic planning project, I'll take everything I've learned from the situation analysis and the positioning development phases and use them to craft a set of strategies for each of the elements of the traditional marketing mix. That means I'll address the issues of communication (advertising, promotion, publicity, etc.), product development, pricing policy, sales and distribution, plus customer service, technical support, and any other relevant function that bridges the gap between my client (a manufacturer or marketer) and the customer base.

The specific vehicles differ greatly from one project to the next, and I don't think I've ever had two projects that were similar enough to be able to simply apply the recommendations from one to the other without significant rethinking. The principles and objectives don't change, just the relative importance of the elements and specific implementation details.

You'll want to deal with the elements of the marketing mix as they apply to your own situation. By the time we consider each of them, you'll understand why the principles are the same whether you're an experienced salesperson who has just been laid off, a CPA who is considering the relative merits of two different public accounting firms, or a senior operations manager who has been "right-sized" out of a job.

Ready to begin? Let's start your situation analysis.

Chapter 3

Where Are You
in Your Professional Life?

The first thing to do when starting any new marketing or strategic planning project is make sure you understand the lay of the land. You want to understand the marketplace, the customer base, the competition, the history, any market research that may be relevant, and the product or service itself.

For a traditional product, this usually involves a visit to the laboratories and manufacturing facilities where product development people can explain the technical intricacies of the offering. It also involves a series of interviews with outside industry experts and people who are intimately familiar with the product category.

You would also want to interview inside experts — the people who are running the company, manufacturing and marketing the product, and tracking its performance. It's important to know what their biases and expectations are, just as it's important to know what the outside world thinks.

Collectively, this in-depth familiarization process is the data-gathering phase of the situation analysis. As we discussed in the previous chapter, it's a mandatory first step in the development of any strategic plan.

And that brings us to the situation analysis for the subject of this book — You.

It's not easy to be objective about yourself

Probably the most difficult part of looking for a job is dealing with the overpowering emotional baggage that accompanies the process. For most people, looking for a job is as unpleasant as getting a root canal. The importance to their lives, though, is so much greater and longer lasting.

And that's only part of the story. Because it's such an unpleasant process, they want to get it over with as quickly as possible. They also want to minimize the pain to their families, and they want to preserve whatever dignity they think they may have left. And they need to attend to their budgeting and financial needs at the same time, because most of us don't have an unlimited checkbook to finance a leisurely job search and still keep up the standard of living to which we've become accustomed.

It's not an easy task when you're both the product and the analyst. There is a formula, or process, though, and we'll be getting to it shortly. The first thing we have to deal with is getting the emotional stuff under control so you're thinking clearly and operating at peak performance. If there's ever a time when you need to be thinking clearly, it's when you're making a major career decision.

So how do we deal with complex emotional issues? How can you structure your thinking so that you're in control, not reacting (or overreacting) to each fear that leaps into your mind?

You have to begin by stepping back and realizing that our culture places career at the center of assessing success in life. If we "fail" at our jobs, we've been taught, we are, in fact, failures. When the *New York Times* publishes an obituary, the headline and first paragraph invariably identify the deceased in terms of his or her work — not hobbies, interests, priorities, or values. Even philanthropists who devote the majority of their adult lives to an avocation or a worthy cause are usually remembered more for their early career accomplishments or how they acquired wealth, fame, or power. Career is obviously what counts.

Further, the acknowledged measure of career success is monetary. We look at the balance in a person's checkbook as the measure of his or her value or net worth. The system is so ingrained we don't even stop to consider other value systems, except as alternative lifestyle issues.

It's no wonder then that when people are out of work — when there's a hiccup in their careers and their income streams are interrupted — they feel that to some degree their value (as individuals who were raised in the career-is-everything culture) has somehow been placed into question. The standard has been predefined in the common culture.

This is a serious emotional issue, as any experienced counselor will tell you. It is not to be taken lightly or dismissed as not being relevant to "my case." A very insightful book by Joe Dominguez and Vicki Robin, called *Your Money or Your Life,* deals with this cultural phenomenon and the resulting relationship we all have with money. In it the authors suggest some alternate ways of defining the roles that careers and finances play in our lives. I recommend that book to everyone — not just those who are in the job market.

Your mission, should you choose to accept it . . .

One important idea to take away from this book is the value of defining and creating a personal mission statement. A personal mission statement is an articulation of what you're all about and what success looks like for you. It includes, implicitly or explicitly, an expression of the values and beliefs that make you tick.

Without such a statement and the thinking that necessarily precedes it, you're bound to find yourself in the out-of-work state many more times over the course of your working life, never feeling like you've arrived.

There's an old adage that cautions "… if you don't know where you're going, any road will get you there." Most of us just keep "going there" without ever thinking about where it is we're going.

With corporate clients I always ask for a mission statement, if there is one, at our first meeting. The mission statement spells out what the company's purpose is, so we'll know exactly what the ultimate goals are and have a basis for evaluating the appropriateness of the positioning, strategies and plans.

If you were trying to get to Los Angeles by hitchhiking, you'd probably never think of taking a ride with someone who's headed for Maine. Yet we change jobs for better pay, improved working conditions, added benefits, perks, titles — whatever — and rarely define for ourselves what success really looks like. When you think of it this way, it doesn't make a lot of sense, does it?

What I'm suggesting is that when you're between jobs, you have a unique opportunity to focus on this critically important issue with more energy and meaning than most of us ever consider devoting to it. And if you do it well, you're more likely to find the right next-job sooner, keep it longer, and enjoy it more than when you simply stick out your thumb and hitch a ride with the next car coming down the career highway.

Chances are, by the way, the reason most people are looking for work in the first place is because they did not do this before they took their last job, and they're now paying the price. It's amazing how people will avoid the planning process in favor of immediate action, even when the evidence of its importance is staring them in the face.

Can't we do this later?

A few years ago I had a new client — the marketing VP for a medium-sized manufacturing company — who was so intent on getting new promotional programs into the field that he wanted to defer the mission statement discussion, the situation analysis, and the detailed planning process until later. He assured me that they wouldn't be forgotten, just delayed a few months.

I was able to persuade him to give me one meeting with the company's senior management team to begin the dialogue on the company's mission, after which I would be a "good soldier" and start on marketing programs while concurrently conducting a situation analysis. It turned out that there was so much disagreement among the senior management of the company as to where they were heading — what their mission was — that everyone asked to continue the process of defining the mission before we did anything else. They were concerned that we'd develop programs that would prove to be in conflict with the mission upon which we'd eventually agree. Even my primary contact who was so eager to begin program development came to realize how important it was to start with a clear understanding of the mission.

When it comes to understanding your personal mission and strategic direction in life, there are a number of ways to approach

33

the matter. There's no single answer that works for everyone, of course, but there are a few useful exercises that will stimulate your thinking.

Graphing your history and outlook

I was once a guest at a seminar in which the group leader had everyone chart his or her life in a very interesting and telling way. We each created a graph in which the x-axis (horizontal) was divided into 7-year blocks of time. At the left side was our age, starting from birth ("zero" on the x-axis). At the right was an age we think we might be when we die — say 98, conveniently selected because it's an even multiple of 7, and old enough that we can't easily project ourselves into that age and situation.

On the y-axis (vertical) we simply placed the numbers 1 through 10, with 10 at the top.

The vertical axis in this graph represents a subjective measure, on a scale of 1 to 10, of our level of happiness and sense of accomplishment (which almost always go together). For each time period in our lives so far, we then selected the number (between 1 and 10) which best rated how happy and fulfilled we were, with 1 being "not at all happy or fulfilled" and 10 being "totally, or extremely, happy and fulfilled." We were asked to start with a value of 5 at birth — in the middle of the range.

We were also encouraged to place notes at the bottom of our graphs to explain the various ratings, and why we felt the way we did in each time period.

One member of our group, Bob L., was a thirty-five-year-old sales manager who was in the midst of a serious job search. He was quite open about what had happened to him and what he wanted next. He shared his personal sense of accomplishment graph with the group, and read his notes to us:

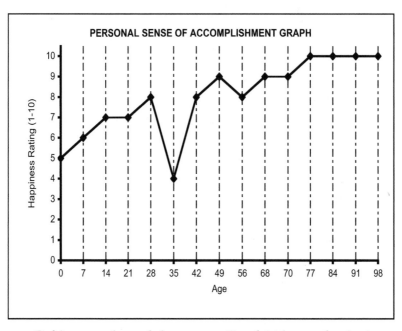

PERSONAL SENSE OF ACCOMPLISHMENT GRAPH

Happiness Rating (1-10)

Age

Bob's notes showed that at ages 7 and 14 he was beginning to get a lot of strokes at school and in extracurricular activities — mostly sports. He had a reasonably successful academic and social life at college from ages 18 to 23. At age 25 he landed his first "real" full-time job, then married at age 26 and got a promotion at age 28. He also became a father at age 29 and listed that as one of the factors that contributed to a happiness rating of 8 at that point in his life.

Then just before his thirty-fourth birthday, a former competitor acquired his company and Bob was let go as part of a right-sizing move. He had been out of work for about six months when he created this chart of his own sense of accomplishment.

You may want to do this exercise yourself, before you read on, so that you can better relate to the phenomenon I'm about to describe. Your notations don't need to be an elaborate story — just a word or two that will be meaningful for you. At the very end of this book there's a blank graph for your personal entries.

And while you're at it, fill in the time blocks for years and ages that lie ahead. Fantasize. Let your dreams take over for a few minutes. How happy and fulfilled will you be ten or twenty years from now? More importantly, why? You may want to make some marginal notes of your reasons.

Bob's notes for future years showed that he expected to get a great job soon, do very well in that job (rising to the level of vice president by age 49), then coast to retirement by age 60. From then on it would be golf, grandchildren, and lots of travel — a 10 on his sense of accomplishment scale. (The slight dip at age 56 traced to Bob's expectation that as he neared retirement, he'd find work a bit less fulfilling.)

Compare your own results

If you spent some time with this exercise, its value is probably quite evident. Most people believe things will get better in the future, and that they were better at some time in the past, than they are right now. This is especially true when there's a "discontinuity" in the all-important career track staring you in the face. (Even if you're just thinking of leaving your job, you probably don't believe you're where you want to be, or you wouldn't be considering a change.)

It's important to address this "attitude" issue head-on, because it is at the root of the emotional (and possibly psychological) problem that is destined to get in your way as you embark on the job search journey.

Let me digress for just a moment to talk about three case studies. I think you'll agree they are relevant to this discussion:

♦ Mitchell S. — Mitchell (not his real name) was raised in a poor family and determined at an early age he would make it his business to be rich someday. He got a great education, including an MBA, thanks to scholarships, loans, and what little help his parents could afford. Once he began his career, he kept changing employers, each time citing the substantial increase in salary as his key reason. He was going to be rich, no matter what the cost. Over a period of fifteen years, Mitchell had five jobs, three children by two ex-wives, at least eight different addresses, a couple of extramarital affairs, and a lot of sleepless nights. He had clearly met his financial goal, as his tax returns showed an income that would place him in the top one percent of wage earners, but he was one of the most unhappy, unfulfilled people I've ever met.

♦ Susan T. — Susan wanted to prove that she could go where no woman had ever gone before. She devoted herself one hundred percent to her job and climbed to a VP level in a large company where there were few women in exempt jobs, let alone in management. She clearly achieved her career goal. But she didn't have time for a social life because every available moment was devoted to her career. On her forty-fifth birthday and her twenty-third year with the company, she realized, probably for the first time, that something was missing — companionship, close family ties, friends. In short, Susan didn't have a life outside of work. And it seemed a bit late to change things.

♦ William R. — Bill was totally devoted to his family and his church community. He probably wouldn't have worked at all if it wasn't necessary to feed and clothe his family. At work, he was a model employee — hard working, conscientious, loyal, and very competent. In fact, his employer offered him major promotions about once each year, always with substantial salary increases. Bill turned them all down though. He didn't want a job that required a lot of travel, or that might entail frequent late nights at the office, or that would have him taking work home over the weekend. Any of these "impositions" would interfere with his priorities — family and church community. By all accounts, Bill was in a dead-end job, with only a little more financial security than a new hire, even though he'd been out of school for almost ten years. He didn't get much credit for career success, but Bill was, and still is, one of the most fulfilled, happy, centered people I know.

Except for their names, these people are real. I know them personally, and I can attest to their career stories and personal feelings of "success."

The point, as you can see, is that career doesn't have to be at the center of your self-assessed worth. It's okay if it is, but it doesn't have to be. You've got to decide that one for yourself.

A game that imitates life

I remember a board game I once played. In it you had to set goals — for fame, power, and wealth — and commit them to paper before play began. Then you amassed points signifying how much of each of the goals you'd set for yourself you'd been able to acquire. The winner was the one who reached his or her goals first.

That game taught two lessons, one good and one not so good. The good lesson is the value of setting personal goals and defining success at the outset. The not-so-good lesson is the implicit suggestion that success consists of some combination of fame, power, and wealth — nothing more or less.

Let's use the good lesson and build on it, without restricting ourselves to a limited set of "success" components. In fact, I would encourage you to think about the priorities in your life and how they impact each other, so that you can define for yourself what the possible goals are and how important each one is for you.

What's important to *you*?

A good way to start is to write down what your personal priorities are. Start with a long list if you like and be honest. No one else will have to see your work.

Here's a core value list that was developed by someone who participated in a career planning workshop a few years ago:

Introspection	Recognition	Respect
Integrity	Compassion	Physical fitness
Creativity	Family	Spontaneity
Thoughtfulness	Serenity	Humor
Spirituality	Insight	Passion

Use this as a starting point and feel free to add or delete as many as you think apply to you. Don't rush. This exercise will provide the foundation for much of what is to come. There's a blank grid at the end of this book that you can use to make your list of core values and priorities.

Once you have your list, try this: narrow it down to just the five most important values. (I simply circled them on my own list.) If you like, you can try to put the most important ones in the first column, or the top rows, to get a head start on the exercise. Don't rush the process. This is an important learning opportunity, and it will serve you well later in the process.

Now that you have the top five identified, see if you can pick just the top three. Again, take your time and really think about your choices. It's not easy to define yourself so specifically and set these kinds of priorities to values you've never questioned before. (I simply put stars next to the five I picked for myself.)

Finally, challenge yourself to select the single most important core value for you. (I placed a second star next to the top item on my list.) Again, don't feel a need to rush through the exercise. It's very important that you give it the time and focused attention required to ensure that the end result is one that really reflects who you are. Your list will probably not look like anyone else's, and your priorities will be your own. It's just for you.

You're probably starting to realize now how truly important this first step is. We're getting to the heart or essence of the "product." We're in the laboratory and we're learning what makes it tick. And we're beginning to frame both the universe of possible jobs (or career moves) and where career fits on your personal priority ranking.

We'll use this list later, but you can begin thinking now about what it means for you. Have you been heading in the right direction up to this point? Is a reassessment in order? Keep this in the back of your mind as we proceed with some additional components of the situation analysis.

Remember, the full situation analysis usually takes four to five months for a product, service, or industry. We don't want to make the assumption that our first interview or trade journal article is one hundred percent correct, and that we suddenly know everything there is to know about the product. We'd rather look at it from a range of perspectives, ask lots of questions, and try different explanations of why things are the way they are.

You owe it to yourself to be just as careful in assessing your core values and doing your own situation analysis. You don't need to take months to do it, but don't go to the other extreme and try to finish the task in fifteen minutes either. Sleep on it. See if you have new thoughts in the morning. Share your thoughts with a close friend or spouse, if you're comfortable with that. In short, give your ideas some time to take shape and refine themselves. You'll be glad you did.

Chapter 4

Where Do I Belong?

At this point, it's probably time to begin to expand the situation analysis beyond the laboratory and relate what you've learned to the relevant marketplace.

Most people, once they get over any initial shock and deal with the trauma of being back in the job market, fall into the trap of searching through the classified ads, stepping up their networking activities, reworking their resumes, and creating a host of busy-work activities to fill their empty days — hopefully expediting the process of finding their next job.

They often have a perceived clock ticking somewhere in the recesses of their minds. "What if I run out of money before I find the next job?" "If I wait too long, I'll become labeled as unemployable." "The perfect job might be gone if I don't seize the opportunity now." You can probably come up with a half dozen more.

The problem with that ticking clock is that it almost always compromises the clear thinking and planning instinct we all know would serve us so much better. And yet we're terrified to take the time to think through what we're doing and make the right decisions for the right reasons.

We're going to take a page from the book on basic marketing to help get over this panic-driven (and perfectly natural) response: **The first thing we have to do is understand our product and our market, and how they relate to each other.** Unfortunately, that's not a quick-fix undertaking, and it doesn't do much to satisfy our needs for immediate gratification. Let's get started though because it's critically important, and the sooner we start, the sooner we'll finish.

Understanding the Product

In the last chapter you developed a list of core values and priorities. Now it's time to relate that list to your career decisions. This time make a list of your personal skills, aptitudes, interests and other characteristics that you believe are assets on the job. These are not values, like the first list, but personal traits and behaviors that you feel are important to success in the workplace.

Here are a dozen possible items for your list — picked from one developed not so long ago by a job seeker I know:

Analytical	Thorough	Loyal
Hard-working	Smart	Precise
Focused	Take direction	Considerate
Articulate	Honest	Risk-averse

Here's a list from another person:

Persuasive	Persistent	Competitive
Sensitive	Intuitive	Alert
High energy	Multi-tracked	Risk taker
Honest	Big picture	Creative

As you can see, they're very different from each other, just as you are different from everyone else in the job market.

Take some time to develop your list carefully. You should be able to come up with at least fifteen to twenty descriptors on your list. If you can't, spend a little more time on it and see if you can at least get a dozen. If you have twenty-five, that's okay. Again, there's a blank grid for this purpose at the end of this book.

Now do the same kind of winnowing you did on the core values list. Narrow it down to the five most important, then three, then one.

You're really starting to define this "product" pretty well, aren't you?

Some people now like to do a similar assessment of liabilities, or potential negatives. I don't think it's helpful in the scheme of things. We all have weak spots or areas that could use improvement, and we usually know pretty well what they are. If you think you would benefit from making that list now, it's okay, but (a) the list doesn't need to be nearly as long, and (b) you don't need to give it nearly as much thoughtful attention. We'll talk about how to handle personal weaknesses or vulnerabilities later.

How do you prefer to think?

There's another aspect of "knowing the product" we need to address now. It's understanding our own preferred modes of thinking, as defined by the late Ned Herrmann of the Herrmann Group. Ned Herrmann did a lot of analysis, based on survey data from more than a million people, of how we each tend to approach problems or situations in life. He even developed a very effective questionnaire that allows for graphic and numerical quantification of your own profile, which describes just how you prefer to solve a new problem or address a new issue. You can read about his research and begin to assess your own style with his book *The Creative Brain*, or the follow-up book *The Whole-Brain Business Book*. The Herrmann Group also maintains a web site at http://www.hbdi.com that explains the approach and offers the survey form (at a modest cost).

This is a highly recommended step in the self-assessment process and one that I believe is well worth the expense. If you're serious about wanting to give yourself every advantage in the job search process, make the effort and spend the money to complete the HBDI — Herrmann Brain Dominance Instrument. The insights it will provide are worth every penny. If you're married, you might want to have your spouse go through the process too.

At a minimum, use the short-form explanation of Herrmann's model provided in the appendix to understand the criteria and begin to form an initial or directional self-assessment of your preferred thinking style.

If you actually submit a form to The Herrmann Group for analysis, you'll have a quantitatively based ranking (high, medium, low) of your preferred modes of thinking, which will serve as a profile of how you approach problem solving and new situations. You'll also find a very interesting comparison of how the seventy-five or eighty possible profiles tend to define people in various careers, or vice versa, based on Herrmann's research.

Understanding the market

The marketplace for your product — you and your services — is the base of potential, or target, employers. Collectively they are your "customer." These potential employers not only have cultures and needs that are compatible with your own, but also have workplace environments where you have reason to believe you will flourish. Once again, it's going to be important to be sure you understand each prospective employer in some depth, and not just spew out hundreds of resumes hoping that somehow, magically, one of them is going to get to the desk of the right person at the right company.

The criteria for selecting your next employer

This homework component can be somewhat more structured than the "product knowledge" exercise. Your public library and the Internet are great places to start. There are some criteria you'll have to have in mind first, though, or you'll chase down a lot of irrelevant leads before you come up with the right ones.

You won't be eligible for a senior marketing job at Procter & Gamble, for example, regardless of your experience or credentials. That's because Procter & Gamble only hires marketing people at the entry level. Similarly, if you want to be a senior manager at Frito-Lay, you have to be prepared to live in Texas, because that's where their headquarters is located, even though they have tens of thousands of people employed all over the United States. And if you want to be at the cutting edge of communications technology, chances are you'll be better off at Lucent Technologies than at General Motors, even though the latter might well have an opening for someone with expertise in communications technology.

This is probably the right place to introduce you to another helpful book, by Richard Nelson Bolles, called *What Color Is Your Parachute?* It suggests some important screening criteria: geography and location, industry, hiring practices, and others. *What Color Is Your Parachute?* is probably the most widely read book on this subject, and it is definitely recommended. Put it on your list of next books to get and use it as a central resource in your job search process.

All of this really boils down to understanding the relevant marketplace and having your own priorities in mind — assessing the product-market fit. Once you've done that, the process of listing the best prospects for your next employer is really quite straightforward.

If location and geography are the most important criteria, you can use the Yellow Pages and local newspapers. Otherwise, some Internet searches and industry publications are the places to start. Don't just run to the help-wanted ads, though, because the challenge is to find the right company, not the first available job. Employers advertise the jobs they need filled now, not necessarily the job that's right for you. Maybe they are the same, but more likely they're not. We're still at the situation analysis stage, remember?

As you gather information on the handful of target employers, try to talk with people who are customers or suppliers of these companies, or even competitors. They can give you insights you might never find in magazine articles, stock analysts' reports, or company literature. Take notes and refer to them often as you go through the homework phase. You'll find that certain ideas tend to repeat themselves — and are probably true — while others have conflicting reports and may bear more scrutiny.

Even if you later decide that these companies are not where you want to work, the insights you gain on them, and the very process of analyzing prospective employers from the standpoint of their desirability as a place to work, will prove to be a valuable asset and resource. Take this assignment as seriously as you would one given to you by your new employer. You don't know how valuable it may end up being.

The client's surprise request

Not very long ago I had begun the situation analysis for a client in the building materials industry. I was actually in Arizona working with a sales rep and meeting some large customers when I got a call from a senior executive at the client firm. He asked me a number of questions about the kinds of things I was learning and the kinds of people with whom I was meeting. At first I couldn't figure out why he was getting so involved in these details at such an early stage in the process. Then he laid it on me.

He was negotiating to purchase another company in the same industry and product category, and the perspectives I had begun to collect on that company would prove invaluable in his negotiations and deliberations. Of course that wasn't an issue that had crossed my mind as I spoke with people in the marketplace, but I could see how my work had an important place in his world, and I was really glad I had taken the assignment so seriously. My input ended up being a critically important ingredient in furthering the client's strategic direction.

You need to proceed with your situation analysis with the expectation that something like this could happen to you.

Where to look for information

If you live near a city in which major employers participate in job fairs, you might consider attending one. These affairs are like big bazaars where companies pay for space to showcase themselves as great places to work, and all the disgruntled employees in the area, along with their out-of-work competitors, pass out resumes hoping that somehow their next dance partner will be better than the last.

From your standpoint, these are wonderful data-gathering events, especially if you are committed to staying in the same area. Just don't get sucked into paying a lot of money for the privilege. There are plenty of job fairs sponsored by the hiring companies who want to make it easy for you to get your resume to them. These are absolutely free. You can really learn the local job market, get a flavor for who is looking for what and confirm (or raise questions about) whatever you've already learned from your research. And don't go to the job fair with the notion that you're going to magically find your dream job there. Go to gather information and "case the joint." You'll be less uptight, and you'll learn a lot more than when you go with high expectations.

Another venue, much better suited to your needs, is the Internet, where there's a virtual job fair going on 24/7, as they say. If you haven't tried on-line classified ads, job recruiting sites, and employers' home pages on the World Wide Web of the Internet, you'll be absolutely blown away with the virtual job market out there. Tens of thousands of jobs are posted in just about every city and town in North America (and the world, for that matter). It makes even the Sunday *New York Times* classified section look like child's play. If you enjoy browsing the Internet, or looking at what kinds of jobs people are trying to fill, you can spend many hours on-line immersed in a kind of job search heaven. Remember though, the assignment right now is not to find lots and lots of job postings; it's to research the marketplace for *your* next (and ideal) job. Use the tools to help you accomplish your objectives. Don't fall into the quick fix trap.

Where Do I Belong?

Only after you've completed your homework should you begin to focus on the details of how you'll select and approach your "perfect" employer.

Chapter 5

Selecting Your Next Employer

Most people don't take the homework, or research, phase of the job search process seriously, so they jump right out of the pan and into the fire, so to speak, by sending resumes to everyone who looks like a possible employer. They eventually get jobs, but not usually jobs they'll remain in for long, so they get to do it all over again in a year or two.

This nonstrategic approach to career planning has even gained some legitimacy lately, as people begin to see themselves as "free agents" in the employment market — like professional athletes who jump from team to team in order to maximize their earnings. This isn't necessarily a bad thing, but it does mean that they'll be going through the uncertainty and inconvenience of moving on a regular basis, and most people, I suspect, would really prefer a more stable work environment. There are enough changes to cope with in our world without losing your rice bowl on a regular basis.

Narrowing the field

This brings us to the process of taking all the research you've done on the marketplace, comparing it to your own strengths and values (as discussed in the previous chapter), and narrowing the list down to a manageable few prospective employers on which to focus your energy.

For most people, this sifting and winnowing process is not terribly difficult. They've usually found five or six attractive candidates and eliminated a dozen others, or at least relegated them to second tier alternatives.

If you haven't been able to get to this point, you may need to do some more homework, or reframe your selection criteria a bit. I know one person who felt very comfortable devising a complex rating system for evaluating prospective employers, and it worked very well for her.

First, she listed 16 criteria that were important to her, and ranked them roughly in order of importance. (She used three levels of "important" — extremely, very and somewhat — as I recall.) Then she assigned a point value to each criterion that matched her ranking — 5 points for "extremely," 4 points for "very," and 3 points for "somewhat."

As she learned about individual companies, she gave them a point ranking for each of her criteria, using a scale of 1 to10. (IBM, in her case, scored a 9 in terms of "good reputation within the industry," for example.) Then she multiplied this score times the importance number ("very," in this example, or 4 points) and recorded the weighted number — 9 times 4, or 36 — on a scorecard for each employer. She then added all the weighted numbers for a prospective employer to get a total score, which could be used to help in her selection of finalists.

This process, it seems to me, is overkill for the assignment and has some inherent assumptions that could, potentially, give a misleading result. If it is helpful for you, feel free to use it, or devise a similar system of your own.

The advantage, of course, is that it forces you to address what's important to you and how each company you're looking at stacks up on each of the relevant criteria. Beyond that, it provides a subtle reminder that you're choosing an employer as much as the employers are choosing you — not an insignificant influence on your attitude, and a perspective that's important to keep in mind at all times.

The most important criterion of all

If you are the type who gets comfort and reassurance from a quantitative assessment, you'll probably like this. If you use it though, be sure that one of the extremely important criteria is your "gut feeling." In the final analysis it's probably the single most important of all the reasons to seek out or avoid a prospective employer.

Intuition — gut feeling, if you will — has long been maligned in business schools and in industry, and it's worth discussing before we move on. As a trained engineer, my schooling was completely oriented toward a rigorous and quantitative approach to problem solving. So was my graduate work in industrial administration, marketing management, and quantitative business analysis. I still find myself using this mode of thinking much of the time.

I discovered somewhere along the way though that intuition — knowing without knowing how you know — is even more reliable than logic and procedure. It's really a great tool we have all been given that's almost always underutilized.

Men, more than women, tend to discount their intuition, and that's for good physiological reason. The corpus callosum, the part of the brain that connects the right and left hemispheres, is bigger, and develops faster, in women than in men. Intuition "lives" in the right hemisphere, and gut feelings are transferred (through the corpus callosum) from that portion of the brain to the left hemisphere for articulation and analysis. In men the transfer medium is more limited than it is in women, so men tend to rely more heavily on more routine, explainable logic and less on right-brain stuff.

Discovering your intuition

By the way, if you haven't discovered your intuitive self yet, you may want to read up on the subject as a kind of self-improvement — like learning a new language or skill. There are a number of good books on intuition, and it's truly a fascinating area for exploration. The one I found most useful is called *Sixth Sense* by Laurie Nadel, with Judy Haims and Robert Stempson. This book also does a nice job of integrating some of the work of Ned Herrmann (discussed earlier) into a better understanding of how your thinking and intuitive processes work.

You may find, as I have, that your intuition is particularly good at solving certain kinds of problems, and once you discover what they are for you, you'll have an extremely valuable tool to use at work or at home, or both.

I discovered, for example, that I could sense pricing strategy issues before they were explicitly defined. I don't know how I do it. It just kind of comes to me. Most clients, of course, aren't terribly comfortable with my intuition as the sole basis for making major pricing decisions that could mean a difference of millions of dollars on their bottom lines. So I developed a rigorous quantitative model that I can use to get the issue of pricing strategy on the table with those clients. It's actually a very neat model that I'd use even if I didn't have a reliable intuition in this area. Once I introduce it to the client, I can begin to ask questions and steer the decision-making process in the direction of my intuition without flaunting it or making clients think I'm some kind of weird psychic when it comes to pricing.

Putting intuition to work

A friend who is a promotion services consultant invited me to a meeting with one of his clients a few years ago. The company is a well-known manufacturer of major appliances, and my friend knew he was outside his area of expertise when the client suggested they discuss positioning and advertising as it related to the work they were doing together. As the meeting unfolded I got this feeling that the real problem was a pricing issue. The client's positioning — their image with consumers and the trade — was that of a high-end product, yet their pricing policy led them to be highly competitive and, in some cases, underpriced. No one said any of this. I just sensed it.

When my friend turned the meeting over to me, I asked a few questions to validate my intuitive feeling. It was as though they'd been waiting for the questions and the discussion that followed. I had successfully put my finger on the crux of the client's single biggest issue within minutes, and we spent the next three hours with four vice presidents (sales, marketing, finance, and manufacturing) discussing a path forward for getting prices in line with their intended positioning. That afternoon was worth tens of millions of dollars on that client's bottom line — and it only came to the surface because I listened to my intuition.

By the way, my friend landed one of the biggest contracts of his career with that company, and to this day they remind him of the tremendous value we delivered that day. Of course, my friend has expressed his gratitude to me in a number of ways, and I'm really glad I could help him and his client the way I did.

The point of all this is that your intuitive reaction to each prospective employer on your short list is not to be ignored in developing your list of finalists. It's one of the more important metrics, if not the single most important one, in my opinion.

It's also worth the time and effort to develop your intuition if you can. Once you learn to trust it, you'll wonder how you ever got along the old way. There's just too much data to analyze, and things are changing too fast to rely solely on traditional logic. If you don't feel comfortable trusting your inner voice for everything, you can always use the traditional backup system — linear thinking — on important matters and with people who are threatened by this unconventional tool.

Chapter 6

Off the Beaten Path

Before we get into using the situation analysis to develop a positioning and strategy set for your job search, it's probably a good idea to look at a few alternatives that may creep into your thinking while you're preparing your game plan. They're worth the time it will take to discuss them because, if we don't, you'll always wonder "what if…"

Should I go it alone?

We've assumed, so far, that you're going to want a traditional job, with an existing company — probably even one that's well known and perhaps publicly held and traded. Certainly that's been the most common scenario in the past.

Things are changing though, and smaller companies are growing much faster than large companies; people are going into business for themselves, working from home, and forming strategic alliances in ways that have not been very popular until now. How does this impact the search for your next job?

As a professional management consultant who works mostly alone, I'm asked all the time about consulting as a career option. The thoughts I'm going to offer on this subject certainly apply to "lone wolf" consulting, but they also apply, for the most part, to any small business that you might start, whether it is a retail business, a distribution opportunity, franchise operation, multilevel marketing, dot-com start-up, or service business.

The good, the bad, and the ugly

Having your own business is a mixed bag. There are great rewards and lifestyle benefits to be realized from "doing your own thing," but there are also some pretty steep prices to pay, sacrifices that will be required, and emotional tolls that will be taken. You'll have to decide for yourself whether you're up for these or not.

Certainly the biggest attraction for most people is that you get to work for yourself. You're in charge, you determine what the priorities are, and there's no one who can ever fire you. If the business is successful, you get the credit (and maybe even a lot of money), and the satisfaction of doing it your own way can be a very high.

On the flip side, the burden is all yours, you are responsible for everything, your reputation is on the line, and you may stand to lose your life savings in the process. That's pretty sobering.

Consulting

Statistics show that the vast majority of new start-up businesses fail within five years — and most of those don't make it much more than a year or two. I've observed this myself with friends and acquaintances who thought they'd like to be "consultants" while they kept an eye on the job market to see if anything attractive came along. In just about every case, they were not able to make a go of their consulting businesses, and the magical "perfect job" didn't show up either. They were back in the job market after a year or two of deluding themselves. (Those of us who have been consulting for ten or twenty years have gotten used to these here today, gone tomorrow consultants, but it always amazes us that people think this business is so easy and attractive.)

Retailing

My friends with retail businesses have an additional complaint: they are tied to their stores almost one hundred percent of the time, and there's not much opportunity to keep a broad perspective on life, business, or much of anything else. A retail business tends to suck up all your waking hours — even when you can afford to hire a good manager. If you're a workaholic anyway, this may not be a big problem. If you're not and don't want to be, it could be a knock-out punch.

Multilevel marketing

MLM (multilevel marketing) operations offer another alternative that has become quite popular. I know a number of people who have given this a shot. Unfortunately, I don't know any who have stuck with it long enough to make it a legitimate career. Most of them keep it as a sideline, a way to make a little extra money or to support their own need to be in management (i.e., keeping their "downlines" motivated and productive). Despite what the promoters would have you believe, I suspect this is not an easy way to make a living. At a minimum, it requires a nonstop, aggressive sales orientation that could be equally productive and rewarding working for a traditional company.

Franchises

Franchise ownership is another alternative, and I know some very successful and happy franchisees. The advantage of a franchise (as opposed to doing everything yourself) is that the product or service, marketing, and operations decisions are already tested and proven. You purchase them by paying your franchise fee. If it's a retail business you're going to be running, then all the same considerations apply that would apply to starting your own retail business. Ditto for a service business. The fact that there's a proven formula in place saves you the pain (and expense) of learning certain lessons the hard way and in many cases improves your chance of beating the odds that are otherwise stacked against you.

The bottom line on all these alternatives is to be sure you're getting good information. Talk with people who have done what you're considering doing and listen very hard to what they have to say. Ask them about the negatives and the frustrations, not just the "good stuff." Do the same kind of in-depth homework you would do on a prospective employer. Understand the industry and know who the key players are, how they make decisions, what drives them, how they go to market, and so forth. Then you'll be able to make an informed decision for yourself.

Partnerships

A popular subset of the "go it alone" approach is "go it alone with a partner." The partner could be a friend, business acquaintance, spouse, relative, or mentor — presumably someone whose knowledge, skills, talents, or know-how you respect and value. If you think this approach is somehow more attractive than going-it-alone "alone," please consider that the track record of successful partnerships is even worse than that for sole proprietorships. That's because, in addition to all the problems and stresses associated with making a business succeed, you have to devote a substantial amount of effort and emotional energy to making the partnership work. It's much more difficult than making a marriage work, and the statistics on that are not exactly encouraging.

In my consulting practice, I often team up with another consultant who, in a sense, is my "partner." Some years, we've done as much as seventy-five to eighty percent of our business in this partnership arrangement — even though we have separate companies and non-shared clients as well. We've discovered some tools and arrangements that make it work for us, but it's not always easy.

For example, everything we do together is managed on a fifty:fifty basis. We're equal partners, or we're not partners at all. This ensures that neither of us feels like we work for the other, or is number two in a two-person relationship. The flip side is that when we don't agree on an issue, there can be days, or even weeks, of tension until we decide on a mutually agreeable resolution. It's interesting that we've been able to turn this into a client benefit on occasion. We present two options to the client, with rationale and supporting arguments for both. We then frame the key decision criteria to the clients and let them decide on a path forward. (Sometimes we even present the options by changing places — I'll present my partner's point of view, and he presents mine.)

The ancillary advantage of our posture with the clients is that when we do agree on a proposed path forward, the clients feel that our point of view should get two votes, because when we disagree with each other, they know we will say so.

Internet-based businesses

I don't think I've had a career discussion with anyone in the last few years without getting to the subject of an Internet-based business early in the session. The Internet is clearly one of the most incredible phenomena in the history of mankind, and it's especially appealing in a climate of knowledge-transfer and service-economy thinking. The Internet is obviously a valuable tool, and a lot of people are going to make a lot of money by properly harnessing and tapping into the magic of cyberspace.

The career options run the gamut of trading stocks or commodities on-line, brokering collectibles on e-Bay (or another auction site), creating a storefront of your own on the web, and designing web sites for others, all the way to using e-mail to spam sales pitches for MLM companies and other get-rich-quick schemes. All of them have the potential to become major money-making opportunities, if that's what you think would really turn you on (and, in some cases, if you can live with yourself).

There are two aspects of Internet businesses that newcomers usually overlook in their excitement. First is the hard-nosed business plan. How is the business really going to make money? What's the ramp-up period? Is the business scalable (i.e., will it work just as well when you have ten thousand hits a day as when you're testing it and have only fifteen hits a day)? Is it really a sound business proposition, or is it something that just seems like it would be fun for a while? What's the plan, or is this just a whim? There are plenty of Internet-based businesses that are highly visible, well conceived, and well run, but they aren't making any money and probably won't for many years to come. That's okay if you have very deep pockets, angel investors, or an IPO ready to go. For most of us it means no income for a while, and that's a scary thought.

Second is the lifestyle question. Are you prepared to work alone? It's just you and your computer most of the time. Everyone else is just an e-mail address or message in your in-box. Most people who try this kind of solitude as a way of life end up hating it after a while. They crave the interaction with live human beings, getting out of the house once in a while, and more. Remember, the Internet is a 24/7 medium, and there are always thousands, or even millions, of people on-line. Do you have the discipline to work in that environment? Is this the lifestyle that matches your personal profile?

I'm not trying to discourage you from becoming the next Bill Gates. I'm just trying to inject a note of sobriety, because I know how alluring the Internet can be as the foundation of a career change. I also know how many people who try to launch an Internet business are quickly back in the job market looking for a more traditional form of employment.

* * * * *

If you are at all interested in some form of "go it alone," or feel a need to get more information, let me recommend that you read several recent issues of *Inc.* magazine. It's the leading trade journal for entrepreneurs and small business owners, and it regularly deals with issues like why a particular business did or didn't succeed, how couples working together resolved their family and business conflicts, financing options for new businesses, unique or innovative partnership arrangements, and so on. These are all issues you're better off addressing before you make the leap, and learning from the experience of others is a great way to steep yourself in the mind-set you'll need. Another worthwhile magazine is *Fast Company,* which has become a favorite of the new wave of Internet-savvy employees, managers, and entrepreneurs.

If you decide to travel an alternative route, you'll undoubtedly want to do a lot of reading and research about the pitfalls and keys to success in your selected career path — the industry, general business and competitive climate, and start-up issues. The balance of this book applies to those who opt to follow the more traditional approach and get a "real" job.

Chapter 7

Your Face to the World

Once you have completed your homework — and not a minute sooner — it's time to think about the strategy you're going to follow in order to land that next job. Chances are you have narrowed the list of prospective employers down to a relatively small number of near-perfect candidates. How do you get them to notice, appreciate, and want you?

This is a classical marketing problem. Think about the question every product manufacturer asks: "How do I get people to buy my product?"

That's a particularly difficult question for manufacturers who believe they are competing in a commodity market, where the only real differentiation between products is price. I've probably dealt with more companies who come from the commodity mind-set than not, and that poses a particular problem right from the outset.

It's relevant to your situation too, because in some ways you might think YOU are a commodity on the job market.

Consider products like milk, canned tuna fish, and potato chips. You can't get much more commodity than those, can you? In each of the so-called "commodity" product categories I've had to deal with, the solution to the problem hinged on the same thing: **there's no such thing as a commodity.**

Commodity is a state of mind, not an inherent attribute of the product. At one level, everything is a commodity. There's nothing you absolutely have to have for which there is no alternative or substitute. At the other extreme, each product offering has something that makes it unique. Let's examine that unique end of the spectrum, because it relates to an important point you need to understand in developing your positioning and marketing strategy.

The difference between potato chips

When I first became director of marketing at Frito-Lay, I marveled at how a commodity like potato chips could have become a highly competitive branded category. After all, I reasoned, potatoes all look alike coming out of the ground, they get peeled and sliced by standard processing equipment, they're fried in various oils (none of which are proprietary), then they're salted, packaged, and delivered to consumers. How can you differentiate one brand of potato chips from another?

It didn't take me long to learn, of course, that all my assumptions about the commodity-ness of potato chips are a complete myth. That was probably when I first realized that there's no such thing as a commodity.

First, there are potatoes and there are potatoes. Some are good for making potato chips and some aren't. Frito-Lay actually developed a special breed of potato and encouraged farmers who wanted to sell to Frito-Lay to use the approved seed for their crop. The resulting potatoes were optimized to provide the right taste, frying characteristics, and yield.

The differences didn't stop there. Freshness is a key determinant of how well you'll like a potato chip. When it's three weeks old, it won't taste as good as when it's only one week old. And if the packaging is inferior, it won't stay fresh nearly as long. A second area of differentiation, therefore, is in raw ingredient logistics, packaging and distribution. Not everyone handles this the same way, and consumers can tell the difference. Frito-Lay has a very sophisticated logistics system for getting potatoes from the ground to their facilities quickly, for packaging to preserve freshness and for distribution to retail stores in record time. A consumer could very easily buy a bag of Lay's potato chips in, say, Chicago, within days of when the potatoes came out of the ground a thousand miles away.

All of this demonstrated to me that a commodity doesn't have to be a commodity if you don't want it to be. I could give similar examples from dairy marketing (milk is milk, isn't it?), table salt (look what Morton's has done with that category!), and a host of industrial products — like TiO_2, nylon carpet fibers, polyester pillow fiberfill, x-ray film, and many more. The list of un-commodity commodities is a long one.

Your potato chip difference

So now let's get back to the question of how you market a product so that the customer base will notice, understand, and appreciate its uniqueness. That's what you want to do for yourself, isn't it?

The answer is to position the product so that it satisfies a recognized and important need of the target audience — or customer — and communicate that fact in a compelling way.

Here's where your homework will begin to payoff.

There must have been a reason why the company candidate list you developed seemed so "right" for you. See if you can articulate the reasons — and be as specific as you can. In most cases, if you were honest with yourself and careful in doing your homework, you'll find that the values you identified as priorities for yourself, and the skills and characteristics you consider personal strengths are exactly consistent with the values and needs of your prospective employers. In fact, if they are not, it's time to reassess the work you did so far. Somehow there's a disconnect, and there's no sense moving ahead with that kind of discrepancy staring you in the face.

Assuming you're comfortable that the fit is a good one, you need to be sure the messages you're going to send to the prospective employer are the right ones. In marketing, we call this "positioning."

Positioning

Positioning is the perception, or image, that the target audience has of a product or service (or company, or YOU). It includes a key thought or two — no more. You can't be perceived as having too many distinct characteristics or strengths because they then begin to read like a generic description of the ideal candidate and lose credibility. Pick the single most important strength or, if you must, two. Resist the temptation to pick three or more. Trust me, it will just confuse things.

Write it down so you're clear in your thinking. You might write "great communicator" and "high energy level," for example. Or you might write "highly analytical" or "very people-sensitive." That's going to become the headline thought and the cornerstone of your positioning.

Next, develop a support statement for the positioning headline. Why should anyone believe that positioning? What's the "reason why" it's true? Write that down too. Cite specific examples or components.

Don't rush this process. In fact, the best positioning statements are usually developed over a period of days (or even weeks) by considering a range of alternatives, synthesizing new ones that include nuances of one or two old ones, which are carefully wordsmithed to communicate exactly the right image or thought sequence.

For example, here's a personal positioning statement a friend of mine developed:

> *Gerald B. is a visionary leader with a solid and proven track record of success. As COO of the XYZ Corporation, he led the company from its beginnings as a privately-held firm with less than $15 million in sales to a publicly traded company with more than $100 million in sales, improving earnings tenfold in a period of just four years.*

Impressive, you say? I can't match that. Not so fast. Let me tell you about Gerry. Everything in his positioning statement is true, but here's some additional information.

Gerry was fired by the XYZ Corporation's CEO because it became clear that Gerry couldn't lead the company going forward. Gerry was a terrible manager of people, and as the company grew, and more employees relied on management for training and direction, the CEO felt he needed a professional manager who could maintain control and motivate people. Those weren't Gerry's strengths. Gerry was a visionary who knew how to take the company public. Once that had been accomplished, Gerry's role was no longer seen as valuable or necessary.

By the way, don't feel too sorry for Gerry. He walked away with several million dollars worth of stock and a very attractive separation package. You can probably understand, however, why Gerry needed some counseling and planning time before he reentered the job market. He'd never thought about his strengths and limitations before. He was too busy doing what he did so well — and so successfully. The homework he did, learning about himself and about the kinds of companies who could use his "product," and the process of proactively positioning himself, were real eye-openers.

How to develop a
strong positioning statement

There are some guidelines about positioning that have withstood the test of time, and they may be useful in developing your positioning statement.

First, positioning has to be truthful and accurate. The target audience is going to get to know you — the product — very well and any exaggeration or misstatement is going to be discovered very quickly. It would be a real "kiss of death" to represent the product as something it isn't.

Next, the positioning should focus on a benefit that is important to the customer (or your future employer). A positioning statement that promises a secondary benefit, or one that isn't really important at all, won't be nearly as persuasive as one that goes to the core of what's likely to be on their minds. As an example, you may be a real stickler for details, and in many jobs attention to detail is critically important. It's usually not the main reason an employer will hire you though, so it's important that you look for a higher level benefit — say, in this case, meticulous accuracy. This includes attention to detail, but expresses it as a higher level benefit.

Finally, the positioning focus should be on a unique and compelling feature — one that only the candidate can deliver and that is central to the company's or the job's success. If you've done a good job of matching your own strengths and values to the company's needs and culture, you can probably deliver on this positioning requirement.

In product and service positioning, we talk about the use of words like "first, best, and only" as signals that this requirement is being met. In truth, it is not always easy and it's sometimes a real challenge in positioning an individual. In some cases, it's only implied, as in Gerry's case, where reference to his "proven track record" suggests that not many people could have pulled off what he did (i.e., "…only Gerry could have done this…").

One more point about positioning: The image you're trying to create for yourself is in the mind of your target audience (or prospective employer). Perception is reality, so if the person you're addressing perceives the positioning value, that's reality for him or her. If you look and talk like a stereotypical used car salesman, that's what you are (in their minds). What your written positioning statement says (e.g., "… thoughtful, professional account manager …") doesn't count. That's why it's so important for the positioning statement to be honest, accurate, and completely truthful. You can't fake who you are — at least not for long.

When you have a positioning statement that you believe identifies and distinguishes you accurately, it will become the cornerstone for all your job-seeking activities. In marketing, we often test the positioning by looking at its implications on the other elements of the traditional marketing mix. In the case of your strategic planning, we're going to come back to the positioning statement repeatedly as we explore strategies for generating awareness, managing initial contact, and getting the offer you want from your target employer.

Chapter 8

Making the Right First Impression

There are three stages any potential customer (or employer) must go through intellectually before he or she will buy your product: awareness, understanding, and preference. If you aren't even known to your next employer, he or she can't possibly consider you. Once the employer is aware of you, he or she needs to understand who you are and what strengths you bring to the party. Then he or she must appreciate why you are the best, or most preferred, available alternative.

Taking your positioning to the market is how you'll generate awareness and at least a modicum of understanding.

The potato chip "lineup"

When I was at Frito-Lay, one of the things we did every Friday morning was convene the senior management of the company in the boardroom to look at and taste competitive potato and corn chip brands from all over the country. They were flown in from virtually every major market and displayed on the boardroom table. If you didn't know what you were looking at, you'd simply think someone had dumped a few cases of chips on the table, then divided the mess into small piles, each near an empty package.

In fact, each bag of chips was carefully opened and displayed near the package in which it came, with the competitive brands adjacent to their Frito-Lay counterparts, which were also plucked and sent from retail shelves in the respective markets. We compared appearance — light, dark, large, small, broken, whole, overcooked, undercooked, everything — salt level, package code-dating, and a variety of technical details (like cooking temperature, which the experts could tell just by looking at the chips).

To a novice, the chips all looked alike. I remember being stunned by the sight of the senior management standing around a table looking at a mountain of chips every week and wondered what purpose this could possibly serve — that is until I began to understand the subtle differences. After a while, even I could pick out the manufacturer just by looking at the chips. I knew that the darker chips came from the Northeast, that some chippers used mostly small potatoes, that salt levels varied by region, and on and on. After a few months, the chips no longer all looked alike.

More important, consumers could tell the difference too. They didn't all share exactly the same preferences, but they knew what they liked and which brands consistently delivered. Ultimately what Frito-Lay management was doing was anticipating what consumers were going to need and finding a way to deliver it to them on terms that were satisfactory to both the consumer and the company. They were *marketing* potato chips.

The potato chip difference

The ability to distinguish between seemingly identical "commodity" products was a great symbolic lesson for me, and I hope I can convey its importance to you and your career planning. It's really at the heart of positioning, and it's one of the most important requirements if you're going to set yourself apart from the crowd — the "commodity" group of people looking for new career options. You have to help prospective employers distinguish one chip from the other.

In today's job market, the resume has become a primary communicator of the positioning — whether it is consciously thought of that way or not. When prospective employers look at a resume — and they probably look at dozens, if not hundreds, of them each year — they form a mental image of the candidate. Either the candidate supplies the image quite literally, or the reader picks up on a few key words or thoughts and does it himself or herself.

The most effective strategy is to control the communication of your positioning as much as you possibly can. If you're convinced the target company is right for you, and you've done your homework thoroughly, there is no reason to leave the reader's understanding of who you are to chance.

The one-of-a-kind resume

Since you're not blanketing the world with copies of your resume, you can — and should — customize each resume for maximum impact on its intended audience. Considering the importance of this "first impression," there's no need or reason to use a one-size-fits-all resume. Put words and thoughts into your resume that will appear to your target audience like rifle shots aimed at the bulls-eye, not a shotgun hoping that somehow something will find its way into your range.

I'm not talking about minor surface changes to a basic boilerplate document. I'm talking about a total re-engineering of your resume for each company you are truly serious about.

Consider these two opening statements of career objectives crossing the desk of the human resource person looking for a new assistant plant manager in a food processing plant:

> *A highly motivated individual seeking a management position with potential for greater responsibility based on performance...*

and

> *An opportunity to learn and master the management of a high-quality food processing plant...*

I submit that the second statement positions the applicant as a quality-sensitive person who wants to learn and perfect his or her skills in the target employer's business and implicitly become more valuable to the employer, while the first one suggests an individual who simply wants to get promoted somewhere. ("...based on performance..." at least suggests that the applicant is willing to *earn* the promotion.)

With your positioning statement in mind and a good understanding of your target audience, you should be able to construct a one-page resume that is guaranteed to leave the reader with a clear understanding of who you are and why he or she should want to learn more about you.

In resumes, less is more

Notice the "one-page" requirement. That's all you get and that's all you should need. Longer resumes suggest you are not focused, don't know what you're trying to communicate, or you're focused too much on what you have done in the past rather than having thought about what's relevant and what you can do for an employer in the future. At a minimum, simply list prior employers and job titles, along with dates of service. If you feel a need for more, a single sentence highlighting your strategically important accomplishments at each employer is probably okay — but no more, and be sure every sentence supports the positioning. If it doesn't, leave it out. No one was ever faulted because his or her resume was too short.

Remember the purpose of the resume: it's to get the interview, not to get the job. Employers don't hire resumes; they hire people. The resume is simply a kind of calling card, or awareness-generating device, that helps position the applicant, and it helps the employer prescreen to get the right applicants to the interview. Here's a case where less is definitely more. One page, decent margins and readable type (never less than 10-point, 12-point is better).

There are lots of books on preparing a resume, and there are software packages that handle the layout and typography for you. If you are really unsure of yourself in this area, check them out. In most cases, the substance of the resume — the information you include about yourself — is so much more important than the form that you're probably better off focusing on what you include, and how you structure what's there, than on formatting and layout.

Professional recruiters and agencies

I know it's common practice to send copies of your resume to every professional recruiter you can find. There are the big, national and international firms, smaller local and industry-specific firms and individuals that do a lot of placement work for major employers. I'm not suggesting that you should ignore these "headhunters." The majority of them do an excellent job of filling the positions their clients assign.

The thing to keep in mind though is that professional recruiters work for the client companies. They are paid to find the right person for a well-defined job. In many cases, they're looking for very specific skills and experiences as prerequisites for the position. The chances that your perfect job and the job they're trying to fill right now will be the same are not very great. And if you keep your resume general (i.e., nonspecific) in terms of what you're looking for, two things can happen when it gets to the recruiter:

- ♦ First, it could be discarded or ignored because they don't see the key words they're looking for in the jobs they're trying to fill.

- ♦ Second, you could end up being a candidate for a job that is off-strategy for you.

Either way, you lose. The chances that your targeted resume will match the specs a recruiter has gotten from his or her client are in the same range as winning the lottery.

If you're committed to broadcasting your resume to every recruiter you can find, this probably won't dissuade you. Go ahead and give it a shot. But don't think you've done very much to insure your chances of getting the right next job. Continue to pursue a vigorous job search on your own. If you end up with a winning number in the recruiter's job lottery, consider it serendipitous.

Don't interpret this as a negative comment about the search industry or the many qualified professionals in the field. As a group they do a terrific job — of serving *their* clients. Just remember who pays their salary, and don't expect them to forget either.

Networking

Another popular approach to advertising your unemployment and finding a good lead for your next job is networking. This is the marketing equivalent of publicity and public relations. Keeping in touch with friends and associates in your line of work is never a bad idea, and you never know when one of them might be helpful in pointing you to a good opportunity.

I would never suggest that you avoid the network. To the contrary, it's an excellent vehicle or venue for gathering information that might lead to your next job. What I would recommend though is that you do all the careful homework about yourself and what you want to do with your career (and life) *before* you position (or mis-position) yourself with the people in the network.

These folks are like executive recruiters in the sense that they only know about the jobs that their contacts and companies have open. The chances that one of those will exactly match your target job are not very high. You want to be sure you're clear in your own mind what you're seeking, so you can communicate it clearly and avoid being seen as a person without clear direction or purpose.

Chapter 9

The Interview — An Opportunity to Deliver on Your Positioning

Once the resume has been prepared and sent (directly or indirectly) to a prospective employer, the next concern for most folks is getting ready for the interview. This is the opportunity to ensure real understanding and appreciation.

I'm going to avoid the temptation to make this a how-to manual on interviewing. What I will do is offer a few thoughts that place this critical step in the right perspective.

First, let's talk about the purpose of the interview. Most people think it's to "sell yourself" to the prospective employer or interviewer. That's certainly part of it, but it's not the whole thing. An equally important purpose is to determine whether the prospective employer is one for whom you really want to work. Do they provide the environment you really want? Are the people who work there the kind of people you want to work with day-in and day-out? Would you be proud to be part of the company? Will your job there be reasonably secure, or is the company likely to be downsizing before too long? How's business?

Job selection works both ways

Here's where we get into what is commonly known as "consultative selling." Try to help your prospective employer solve one of his or her most important problems. Let the job offer be an outcome, not the overt objective.

You should demonstrate that you're not desperate for just any job, but that you have some criteria for selection yourself. See if you can take the lead by acknowledging up front that you would like to make the most of the time you have with the interviewer. Suggest that you divide the time between answering the questions the interviewer might have for you and the ones you have for the interviewer.

This does several things for you. First, it demonstrates that you are selecting a prospective employer as much as they are selecting a prospective employee. It communicates that you're keeping control of your own destiny and not simply "begging for work."

Second, it helps structure the time you're going to spend together. If the interviewers are any good, they may already have planned something like that, in which case you're reinforcing the wisdom of their decision and putting yourself "on their side of the table," at least for the hour or two you'll be together. If they haven't thought about it, it's probably going to be reassuring to them that someone has. At a minimum it suggests that you are aware of the need to manage your time well and be considerate of theirs.

Third, it's going to give you a chance to demonstrate your understanding of their company and industry, of business in general and of how you're likely to conduct yourself in a new situation with customers, fellow employees, suppliers, and others. You're going to be prepared, of course, and ask some insightful questions. They'll notice this, and it will be part of their assessment of you — guaranteed.

Fourth, this approach is going to give you a real opportunity to begin to form a bond, or a professional relationship, with your interviewer. You're going to feel more comfortable sharing your thoughts, ambitions, and relevant personal information with someone you consider to be a peer than you would with a person you feel is judging you. The interviewer, too, will probably be a lot more open with you if he or she senses that kind of relationship developing. Ask about the backgrounds of the people interviewing you. How did they end up where they are? How do they like it? What are the favorite parts of their jobs? What are the company's biggest problems? How do they see the future here, and what's their opinion of the way things are going?

Finally, it will give you a legitimate opportunity to determine whether your homework was well done and whether you really want to make a commitment to the target company. Just because you selected it initially doesn't mean you can't change your mind as you gather more information. You're in information gathering mode just as much as they are.

All that said, you still want to present yourself in the best possible light. Even if you later decide this isn't the company for you, you'd at least like to have that option, and if your interviewer nixes you from the outset, that's not going to be the case. So how can you be sure you're presenting your story in the most positive way?

I'm going to let you in on a secret. I learned it years ago from a mentor and a great book. But you won't find it in any of the popular books on how to interview your way into a job.

A "Fear-ful" approach

In the late 1950s, or early 1960s, a man named Richard A. Fear wrote a textbook on the selection interviewing process. (It was last updated in 1990 with a coauthor, and its title is *The Evaluation Interview*.) The book's purpose was to improve the effectiveness of interviewers and interviewing techniques at hiring companies, and Fear came up with a highly structured approach that became known as the "Fear interview." ("Fear" is his name, remember?)

It has proven to be highly effective for companies whose interviewers are trained in the Fear approach, but it also suggests a great way for the interviewee (that's you) to prepare for the interview. Even if your interviewers aren't familiar with the Fear process, chances are very high that elements of it will be part of their approach. If it isn't, maybe you'll even find a way to steer things in that direction and teach them a thing or two about effective interviewing.

The basic premise in the Fear interview is that leopards don't change their spots. You are essentially the same person you've always been, and you're probably going to continue to be that person after you begin working for your next employer. Five years from now, if you take this job, they'll be able to look back and say, "We should have known all along that you would perform this way, because it's obvious from all that happened before you came to work here."

What Fear suggests is that your behavior patterns began to show themselves back in high school and college, and they became more and more evident in your first (and subsequent) jobs, community activities and avocations. If the interviewer can accurately identify the behaviors and traits you've exhibited, and compare them to the needs of the company, he or she will be able to make a decision about you that has a very high probability of being right.

Let's recognize right now that most interviewers are not that sophisticated. They're doing a version of "dating," leading up to a "marriage proposal." This is as much about first impressions as anything else. But that doesn't mean you have to be just as naïve. You can begin to sow the seeds and "teach" them how they should be evaluating you.

Fear suggests that the best way to "break the ice" and get a first look at your behavior patterns is to have you talk about your work experience, starting with the your very first job and working forward to your most recent job. The interviewers should be looking for things like your attitude toward your work, how you regard your employer and former employers, how responsibly you acted, whether you became a leader or a follower on the job, and so forth.

Those are the things, he hypothesizes, that don't change over time. You may be talking about your accomplishments, but skilled interviewers are going to be listening for clues about your teamwork approach (does the prospect say "I" or "we" most of the time?), the importance of your work in your own life, how you handled difficult situations, and so on.

Your job, of course, is to honestly anticipate and reflect those implicit questions or issues and convey an accurate picture of yourself that will help the interviewers realize that you are the right person for the job and the company — if, in fact, you really are.

After you've talked about your work experience to the point where the interviewers have a good sense of your key personality and behavior patterns, Fear would have them check or validate those observations by asking about your formal education. As you describe that, any discrepancies (to the behaviors on the job you described) will be noted. If you were a C student with no activities or outside interests in college, how is it possible you became such a dynamic leader in your first job? Or conversely, if you were captain of the football team in high school, participated in all the intramural sports in college, graduated with a B+ GPA and were president of your fraternity, how does it compute that you've become an introvert or a complainer at work?

You get the idea. Fear suggests that your behavior and personality patterns have not and will not change. The interviewers' challenge is to accurately identify them and match them to the requirements of the job you're seeking. Not a bad idea and one that you should do before you get to the interview.

Fear then suggests that the interviewers look for family or early childhood explanations for the patterns they've identified. Are you an only child? How did you relate to siblings? Adults? Authority figures (like teachers or police)? Did you have lots of extracurricular activities as a kid? Were you an athlete? A musician? What did you do when you weren't in school? How did you spend your summers?

Finally, Fear suggests the interviewers probe for your personal goals, values, and motivators. What drives you? Where are you going with your life? If the interviewer has done a good job of exploring your work history, education, family, and early childhood experience, this last area should be quite evident. If there are discrepancies, dig deeper. Something isn't quite right.

I'd submit that the best preparation you can have for a job interview is to role-play (with a friend or alone) the Fear interview process, and ask yourself if you're comfortable with the job you're going after and your personal match for it. When you're satisfied that it all "computes," you're ready for the interview.

If the interviewers don't do a very good job of structuring a Fear interview, maybe you can do it for them, leading them to the conclusion that you really understand who you are, where you're going, and how well you fit with their culture and needs. And you will be able to give them specific examples of how you've demonstrated the relevant personality and behavior patterns in the past, so nothing is left to chance.

This is probably more than you, or they, bargained for, but it's an important part of the strategy that's going to get the right job for you, so you don't have to go through this every few years for the rest of your life.

Be prepared — an apt motto

One more thing many have found useful: do additional advance research on each company you interview. Shop for their products and services as though you were a prospective customer. Visit their site on the World Wide Web of the Internet. See if they've been in the news lately. Talk to people who are familiar with the company. See if your stockbroker has any information on the company. In short, prepare yourself for the interview as well as you can. If you've done all your homework thoroughly, there's no reason to have any outcome other than the one you want.

Chapter 10

Creating Your Potato Chip Difference

If you've done the right homework, created an effective positioning and prepared yourself well for the interview, you've already gone a long way toward setting yourself apart from the other applicants who want your next job.

In the marketing mix for a traditional product, manufacturers constantly try to come up with novel inducements, called "promotions," as incentives to purchase immediately, engender loyalty to a familiar brand or company, or give customers a memorable way to recall their product or service.

In consumer packaged goods, promotions are the cents-off coupons, sweepstakes offers, buy-one-get-one-free offers (affectionately known by the acronym "BOGOFs"), and the mail-in and special in-package offers that have become so familiar to every shopper who has ever set foot in a supermarket.

In business-to-business situations, there are trade shows, spec sheets, loyalty programs (like frequent flier miles), special "dating" (or extended payment terms), sales contests, gifts (also known as "spiffs"), and other promotional devices that accomplish the same thing.

So how can you take a page from that book and set yourself apart from other applicants? Surely you don't want to be seen as a shameless huckster when your positioning is so much more businesslike, reserved, and ethical.

Actually, differentiating yourself is a very important ingredient in the job search strategy, and one that could very well be a clincher. If all other things are equal, it could get you the job. If the alternative is to hire no one, it could flip that decision and put you in the driver's seat.

There are a couple of ways you can stand out from the crowd and establish yourself with a unique, on-strategy way for the interviewers to remember (and appreciate) what you have to offer.

Free samples are irresistible

The first way is with a "free sample." You've undoubtedly received free samples in the mail, with your Sunday newspaper or from a paid demonstrator in the supermarket aisle. It's probably the most effective way to get someone to try a product. After all, there's no risk.

Why not consider some form of free sample for your interviewers, so they can experience the way you think and perform, with no risk? In consulting we do it all the time.

In almost every case, you can take the homework you've done on the target employer's business and demonstrate exactly how you would handle (or would have handled) an obvious problem or business challenge that's facing the company. Of course there's a chance that you'll be so far off base that they'll laugh at you. That's okay. If you've missed the mark by that much, chances are you haven't done your homework very well, or if you have, they won't appreciate your insights once you are on the payroll any more than they did during the interview.

This approach is seen by some as being high risk, inasmuch as you're going to put yourself in a position of being judged on your important skills, creativity, and thinking ability. My own view is that, if you don't have the confidence to put yourself on the line and do a thorough pre-interview assessment of the employer's business, you don't belong at the interview in the first place. You still haven't identified the right product-market fit for yourself, and you've put the horse before the cart in your job search process.

There are some how-to tricks to help make sure you're on the right track, of course. You can "mystery shop" for the products and services offered by your prospective employer and its key competitors. Mystery shopping is pretending to be a potential customer for the product (or service) and requesting literature, talking to distributors, checking references, and so forth — just as you would if you were really considering a purchase.

You'd be amazed how much you can learn this way, and you'll be just as amazed at how valuable your newly acquired knowledge is to the target employer. It's the rare manager who believes he knows enough about the way the competition operates, the way customers perceive the products or services, or the way distributors (or resellers) present products to prospective customers. That means your homework can have legitimate value to your prospective employer and that can very quickly set you apart from the crowd — a real differentiating vehicle for you.

If your prospective employer's products are available at a retail store, you might consider taking a number of snapshots of the retail environment, including any point-of-sale materials in the category, competitive merchandising techniques, and others. Everyone likes to see pictures of their kids, and to a manufacturer, the product is truly a "kid." One caution: be sure to ask permission from the retail store manager before you start snapping pictures. Some store managers are instructed to prohibit any picture taking without advance corporate approval.

Even if you do not expect to be directly involved in sales or marketing, the information you've gathered and the analysis you've performed will be seen by your employer as a kind of "added value" you bring to the table. It demonstrates like nothing else can that you go beyond the required standards of performance, take an interest in whatever you do, and have made more than the minimum investment in the target company. All in all, you'll stand out from the crowd with your "free sample."

Can we date first?

There's another possibility for your sales promotion. You could offer to work at the company for a few days or weeks, with no obligation in either direction to continue beyond the agreed period. You might not like what you see, and they might not like what they see. Either way, you both get a chance to date before you decide whether marriage is a viable option. I've seen this work with salespeople who ask if they can work with counterparts in other territories before they make a decision (and before the company has to make a decision about them), and I've seen it work in accounting and auditing jobs. If the company is really interested, this could be an excellent way to showcase your "perfect" product-market fit. It has been particularly effective in smaller companies where the position is seen by management as a major, high-risk decision for them.

There may be other possibilities for on-strategy differentiating efforts, but these are the ones that seem to have most value to prospective employers. Your objective is to be genuinely helpful to the prospective employer in assessing you (as a future company employee) and to provide a no-risk opportunity for an in-depth evaluation by the target company.

Check my references

While we're on the subject of no-risk evaluations, we should consider third-party references to be another opportunity to distinguish yourself. You should be prepared to offer your prospective employer the names and phone numbers of a few individuals who can provide information about your work and work ethic. Remember that a former employer can't do this very well. Their hands are tied by legal and ethical constraints. All they can do is verify that you were in fact an employee. Any more than that can get them in trouble — especially if it's less than totally positive.

A better approach is to get individuals with whom you've worked — customers, clients, suppliers, outside consultants, co-workers who have moved on themselves, even former competitors who respect your abilities — to agree to act as references. They're free to offer their views, when asked, without fear of legal repercussion. Of course, you'll want to speak with them first to be certain they aren't uncomfortable in the role. If they have any reluctance, don't push it. They're probably not going to be your best references.

A final note about differentiation: resist the temptation to make your "promotion" a price reduction. Don't offer to work at half the regular salary for a few weeks or months. It depreciates your value and signals a kind of desperation that will scare most employers. If the only thing that separates you from other applicants is the fact that you're willing to work for less, you have a serious problem in assessing the product-market fit, and you should rethink your whole plan. As we'll discuss in Chapter 11, compensation is something you shouldn't have to compromise; that would be off strategy.

Just stick to your plan and do everything you can to demonstrate your value, or potential value, to the prospective employer. Go out of your way to show your genuine interest in his business, the seriousness with which you take your job and your career, and the core values and skill set you bring to the party. If the match is right, they'll recognize it too.

Chapter 11

Avoiding Common Pitfalls

By far the most common pitfall that most job applicants fall into is not keeping their "edge" or familiarity with important changes in their industry, job function, or the general business climate.

In most cases, it's no small task to remain current with the latest technology or technical know-how, the changing regulatory climate and changes in industry practices. You're constantly changing just to keep up with the requirements of your job.

When you're looking for your next job, though, it's important to demonstrate — to yourself and your prospective employer — that you will make a sincere and serious effort not to fall behind the curve.

Set some additional goals to see if you can separate yourself a bit from the pack by adding some skills or knowledge that everyone else may not have. This is a longer-range strategy and not something that you can easily do to impress your next employer, if you haven't already begun. That doesn't mean it shouldn't be on your plate though, because it can really make a difference in your value — and to your future worth as an employee.

If you're not computer fluent, for example, it's probably worth some investment of time and money to learn the basics. Word processing, spreadsheets, scheduling, contact management, and accounting are all application areas where, more and more, employers are expecting at least basic familiarity and fluency. Hands-on computer usage is no longer restricted to secretaries and techies, and effective Internet use has become mandatory in most companies.

Similarly, management philosophy is evolving, so that promotable (and hire-able) managers (and wanna-be managers) need to be familiar with the latest thinking. When *In Search of Excellence* was first published, no one had thought much about "management by walking around," even though today it's a commonplace style and MBWA is a familiar acronym. Just knowing what the latest management techniques and thinking are will keep you growing and improving, so a visit or two to the library or bookstore would probably be in order.

You'll feel very smart — and well prepared — if an interviewer asks a question, or raises an issue, and you can respond by saying "There was an article about that just last week…" or "Peter Drucker might have suggested an alternate approach, because…"

If you'd like to become conversant in general management issues fairly quickly, you can subscribe to and read any of the major business publications (i.e., *Fortune, Business Week, Forbes, The Wall Street Journal,* etc.), or more scholarly journals like the *Harvard Business Review.* You can also pick up books by any of the well-known business scholars — like Peter Drucker (management) and Theodor Levitt (marketing), to name just two. And, if you haven't read Steven Covey's *The 7 Habits of Highly Effective People*, I'd recommend it as a must item on your list of continuing business education books.

If you have a technical specialty that has its own journals, periodicals and books, by all means keep up with them. You never know which interviewer will place high value on your knowledge of state-of-the-art practices, and you might even learn something that will be of value in the performance of your job.

Finally, if there are areas in which you feel you could use further personal development, by all means pursue self-improvement courses — either at continuing education facilities near where you live or via some home-study alternative.

Judging a book by its cover

In marketing, we pay a lot of attention to packaging. Packaging is the first-impression appearance of the product — in this case, how you dress, how well groomed you are, how well you listen, how perceptive you are, whether you take notes during a meeting, and so on.

Imagine that you turned off the sound during a television program and could only form opinions about the characters by watching them in action. How much would you know about their personalities? Could you tell that Fred Mertz was more conservative and reserved than Lucy? Would you know that Ed Asner's character on the old *Mary Tyler Moore Show* was a demanding boss? Would you notice the difference in cleanliness and organization between Felix and Oscar in *The Odd Couple*?

Of course you would!

Keep in mind that your interviewer is going to observe a lot about you before you ever open your mouth. Of course, you've got to be yourself, because there's no point in trying to fool someone for whom you're going to be working. They'll learn the truth soon enough. But you want to be certain that you've picked a target company that's comfortable and compatible with your own style and values, and then you want to be sure your "packaging" communicates that perfect fit.

Now let's turn the sound on in that television program, but cover the picture with a dark cloth, so that we can't see a thing. What kind of an impression do you form now?

There are a lot of well-educated and otherwise competent people who still have a high level of anxiety when they are asked to write a formal document, make a speech before a large group, or prepare a presentation for senior management (or an important customer). They know their material, but they've never had the proper training in presentation skills, and they're terrified of the prospect that they'll "look stupid" in front of a boss or important customer.

If you doubt this, look at the success of a home-study program called *Grammar For Smart People*, with which I became involved as an investor and advisor several years ago. In crisp, newsletter format, it teaches communication skills through an entertaining series of "grammar lessons." The target audience is well-educated management types who don't feel they've quite mastered these skills. Thousands of individuals and hundreds of employers in the United States, Canada, and as far away as Asia, signed up for the course, and the satisfaction rating among those who completed it was through the roof. It has even spawned a series of seminars and related products — including a technical writing course, a book on persuasion skills (i.e., selling your ideas), and others.

If you think you have a potential weakness in this area, the time and money spent on a home study program to address it will payoff for you almost immediately. Besides, if your interviewer is highly sensitive to, say, proper grammar and word usage, you could deal yourself a knockout punch by making an unintended gaffe and signaling to the interviewer that you're not well qualified for the job, even though your technical skills are superb. People who have developed these skills often tend to judge those without them harshly, without even being aware of that tendency.

In short, use the time you have to do some reading, studying, and learning that will stand you in good stead with your next employer. The fact that you've taken the initiative in this area will impress most interviewers, considering that they probably haven't done the same in their own careers.

Chapter 12

Show Me the Money!

When it comes to your compensation package, you want to maximize your long-term earning capacity by delivering value that your employer perceives to be greater than your cost. You also want this to be a long-term relationship, with a "repeat purchase" rate that will last until you're ready to retire or change careers. The challenge is to determine a compensation package that is fair for both of you and that will accomplish both of these objectives.

In many cases, the going price for a job will be in a very narrow range, and this will not be an issue. In other cases, you may be asked for your salary requirements or salary history, and you'll need to make a decision. What *are* my requirements, and do I want to let the prospective employer know how little I would *really* take?

Let's start with your salary history. I'd be totally honest about that. If you think it suggests that you'd "work cheap," it's okay to indicate that you are looking for a meaningful increase in your next career move. Just be sure you have a rationale that's reasonable. If you're concerned that it's so high that you'll price yourself out of the "perfect job," it's okay to indicate that money isn't the primary criterion for selecting your next job. Either way, a serious target employer will probably respect your honesty and negotiate in good faith. If they won't, maybe this isn't the company you really want to work for.

If, or when, the discussion does get around to what you think the right salary level is, or what you'd require in the way of salary, my approach would be to use your most recent salary as a starting point. Tell the interviewer what you are (or were) making at your current (or most recent) job and offer a comment about whether that's the level you think is appropriate for the new job. I'd also add something to the effect that "I hope it will very quickly become evident that my value to the company far exceeds my salary level, and that I represent an important asset to the company based on my performance."

Don't forget too that benefits, bonuses, stock options, periodic salary reviews, and job perks are all part of your compensation package, and don't get hung up on a base salary number without considering the total picture.

Most of the time, it has been my experience that salary is not a deal-breaker. Most employers understand that you "get what you pay for" when you hire an employee, and they are not eager to go bottom fishing for employees who can help the company reach its objectives. Similarly, most employees understand that money isn't everything, and that having a fulfilling and satisfying job is worth a lot more than the next incremental dollar of take-home pay.

There is a technique I'll share with you that I've used and seen used very effectively when an employer wants to close the deal with a prospective employee. There are a few instances I've heard of when the applicant uses the same technique, in reverse, to land a job. This only applies when both parties are sensing that the relationship is going to work and the only remaining issue is to agree on a compensation package.

Closing the sale

As the last interviewer of the day, when all the others have agreed that we want to hire the applicant, I would ask the applicant a final question:

> *Are there any remaining questions that need to be answered, or issues that need to be resolved, that would keep you from accepting our offer on the spot, assuming it is fair from a money standpoint?*

If there are, I deal with them, then repeat the question. Eventually, most applicants will say no — all questions and issues have been dealt with. Only money remains.

At that point, I would confirm that if I were to make an attractive compensation offer, the applicant would accept on the spot. With that confirmation in hand, I'd ask the applicant what other offers he or she has, and what he or she would consider to be a fair base salary, considering all the benefits in the package. Almost always, the suggested fair base salary was less than I was prepared to offer, so I'd add a small amount (usually less than five percent of the stated fair number), make the offer, and congratulate the person on getting the job — all in the same breath.

The advantage of this was that these people wouldn't go home and think about how to get a little more, try to play one offer off another, or move on to another company to see whether they could do better. I wanted to close the sale as part of making the offer.

The reverse version of this is would be for you (the applicant) to ask the last interviewer when you might expect to hear from the company, and if there is anything you could say or do to accelerate the process, since you'd like to make a decision as soon as possible. You might then indicate that you are sufficiently convinced that the fit between your needs and those of the company is so good that you'd commit on the spot if the dollar offer were competitive or acceptable — and end your job search immediately.

If the interviewer is unwilling or unable to do this, you might ask what the process is and whether you might talk to the decision-maker yourself. This enthusiasm for a company and a job is something most employers don't often see from an applicant, and it just might work — if you really mean it. Once again, I'd only recommend this if you're being totally honest with yourself and the target company, and if you sense that an offer will be forthcoming.

By the way, when I was using this approach to close the sale as an employer, the smartest applicants would respond with:

> *I'm ready to accept your offer now, but I'd really appreciate a day or two to think it over (or talk with my spouse), and be sure I'm totally comfortable with everything before I accept officially. Would that be okay?*

Of course, I'd never say no to that request, and I don't remember anyone ever coming back to ask for more money in those cases, either. (Remember, I would always try to top their fair number.) I think I actually closed one hundred percent of the people in this category — generally within a few days.

Chapter 13

Handling Tough Questions

So much for the specific elements of your job search strategy. We touched briefly, earlier in this book, on how to best present your strengths, and I promised to address dealing with your weaknesses later. Now it's time to think that through in more detail, because the subject is quite likely to come up in the interviewing process. In fact, self-assessment of your weaknesses is a favorite request of interviewers, as it saves them from having to think too hard themselves when they analyze what they heard and observed at the interview.

The Self-Assessment

Everyone knows that we all have strengths and weaknesses. Otherwise we'd all be perfect and the interview would be meaningless. The question is how to acknowledge your weaknesses in an interview without looking like a worthless dolt who can't do anything right.

This is where I would recommend using the results of your Herrmann Brain Dominance assessment and the analysis of it provided by The Herrmann Group. The "brain map" gives you a convenient way to describe yourself objectively, get full credit for your strengths, and explain your approach to areas that are less comfortable for you.

If you can, it's probably a good idea to explain the tool to your interviewers first. With any luck, they've either had their own thinking profile assessed by Herrmann or will become involved in the process with you to the point where they understand the brain profile mapping approach quite well.

Herrmann defines four modes of thinking or problem-solving which all of us use to some degree. In very general terms, they are analysis-logic, process-procedure, interpersonal communication, and vision. (Don't rely on these labels as a replacement for understanding the meanings. I'm just inserting them here so we can play through an example.) They represent the overlap of left brain or right brain thinking with use of the neocortex or limbic portions of the brain. (Don't worry about what all this means right now. It will all make sense when you've had a chance to read one of Herrmann's books.)

Each person will have at least one quadrant (or mode of thinking) that is his or her "preferred" mode. Other quadrants (or modes) would then be "comfortable" or "avoided." Based on your individual profile — the degree of preference you exhibit for each mode of thinking — it is possible to describe how you tend to behave in problem-solving situations. If there are modes you tend to "avoid," you can explain how you compensate or handle situations that would call for that mode of thinking.

Most people, according to Herrmann, have two or three pre-ferred modes of thinking, and one or two comfortable modes. Only people who are extremely strong in one or two modes would nor-mally have an avoid mode, and the strongly preferred mode usually compensates.

Let's suppose your preferred modes of thinking are analytical-logical and visionary, you're comfortable with interpersonal communication, and you tend to avoid process-procedure. When the interviewer asks about your weaknesses, or areas in which you have some difficulty, you might explain the Herrmann assessment approach, then share your own profile, with an explanation like this:

> *I tend to be very analytical and logical, and I also gravitate toward holistic, big picture approaches to solving problems. I've never had any problem working with and through people, and, in fact, I am very comfortable in situations where communication is key. The area I have to watch out for is following established procedures and getting the process to work for me. Of course, I recognize how important this is in any organization, and I've been able to compensate for my natural tendency to avoid dealing with process issues by working closely with people who are strong in this area. I genuinely appreciate the value these people bring, and I have been able to largely overcome my own aversion to process and procedure matters by listening to and working closely with them.*

I think you get the idea. This approach responds to the question, recognizes explicitly that you have a weakness and explains how you deal with it in a workplace situation. It places the weakness in proper perspective and communicates that you are able to be objective about your own performance attributes.

Having this objective measure of your thinking profile allows you to discuss strengths and weaknesses in a way that doesn't need to make you feel defensive. After all, *how* you think isn't something you can generally change, and using the Herrmann assessment offers a picture of your weaknesses that won't cripple you in an interviewer's eyes. It also lets you talk about your strengths at the same time you deal with weaknesses, often mitigating anything that might otherwise be a problem.

There are obviously other ways to deal with the sensitive area of weaknesses, but I have not come across any that address the issue in as objective and positive a way as the Herrmann Brain Dominance Instrument.

Work History

Another area that is sensitive for most people is their work history and their reasons for leaving prior jobs. After weaknesses, this is probably the most commonly asked tough question by un-skilled or semiskilled interviewers.

There was a time that moving from job to job was considered a serious negative in assessing job candidates. It suggested there was something about the individuals that would make them less desirable in a new job and indicated that they probably were not going to be long-term, committed employees. There are still a lot of people who believe this, and they are making important hiring decisions. There's a basis in truth for their concern, so if you've had more than one job so far, it's important that you prepare yourself for questions in this area.

Let's begin our discussion of your job history with two important rules:

- Don't ever tell a lie, and

- Don't bad-mouth a previous employer.

The rationale for these two rules should be obvious, but they are so important I'm going to expand on them anyway.

I cannot tell a lie

The first rule — don't ever tell a lie — is more than a platitude about ethical behavior. It addresses one of the few potential knockout punches in your effort to land the job you want. No employer is going to hire someone they believe to be a liar. Would you? Remember that anything you say to your prospective employer becomes fair game for verification in reference checks. Getting caught in a lie won't do much for your chances of getting an offer.

Let's say you tell a "little white lie" in the interview process, it doesn't get picked up during reference checking, and you get the job and go to work for the employer. Then a few months down the road, someone at your new company learns something that suggests you might have been less than totally truthful during the interview process. Suddenly there's a taint surrounding you, people begin to question your honesty, and you're playing defense every day at work. How long do you think that's going to last? How are you going to feel facing your coworkers and management then?

You get the idea. Lying is simply not worth the risk. In some cases, there could even be legal consequences, though I'd hope you never try to test those waters. It's much safer all around to tell the truth.

When Peter talks about Paul ...

The second rule — don't bad-mouth a previous employer — goes back to an old adage that says: "When Peter talks about Paul, you learn more about Peter than you do about Paul." When you say anything about a previous employer that is anything less than complimentary, you are essentially telling the listener that you (a) have no qualms about denigrating an employer (including your next employer), and (b) had the poor judgment to work for someone you didn't respect.

So what do you say if you got fired by a jerk of a boss at your last job because you did something you thought was right, but he or she didn't like? You need to be honest, and you don't want to bad-mouth your employer.

My strong suggestion is to be very up front about the fact that you were fired. That's the easiest thing to verify, and this information is most likely to be questioned for verification if you try to conceal it. I'd also suggest that you explain, in a convincing manner, why your previous employer was justified in firing you, so that it's clear you understand what happened and have no bitterness about it. Only then should you explain your side of the story, why you did what you did and why you thought, at the time, it was the right thing to do.

By presenting the employer's side of the story first, and supporting it in a way that shows you respect the decision, you avoid entirely the potential bad-mouthing, which might be anticipated. You demonstrate that you can be objective about these kinds of emotional issues, and you avoid any potential for backbiting or revenge. It's the only way to make the best of an unfortunate situation.

If there's a generalization that can be drawn from the suggested approaches to these two situations — the self-assessment and job history issue — it's that you need to be an objective reporter of the facts, not a defense attorney. Any embarrassment that might result during the interview will certainly be less painful than the outcome of any other alternative.

There are undoubtedly other tough questions you might face from an interviewer who is determined to trip you up. The best advice in those cases is to follow the rules and remain objective in reporting history, without necessarily laying blame, establishing fault, passing judgment on others, or assessing responsibility.

Chapter 14

Accepting the Offer

Getting and accepting the job offer — that was the objective, remember? — is the payoff for all the homework, positioning, strategizing, and job search thinking and effort. And, as any experienced salesperson will tell you, the best transactions are win-win arrangements. Both parties benefit from the relationship.

This certainly applies in your job negotiation. If your employer, two or three months after you start, feels he or she has been sold a bill of goods, neither of you has won. That's why honesty is so important up front. On the other hand, if you've both been honest and open with one another, there should be no surprises and you'll both be winners.

Your job, as the salesperson for your product — you — is to ensure that the prospective employer understands the product accurately and truthfully, and that the product — you — can really deliver on the promises you've made in representing it.

The Potato Chip Difference

If you've never done any selling professionally, it wouldn't hurt to read a few of the better books on selling, though that may be overkill if you really get into this total process. The two books I've found most helpful, should you want to do a bit more reading in this area, are *Strategic Selling* and *Conceptual Selling*, both by Robert B. Miller and Stephen E. Heiman. They deal with the sales process in complex selling situations, where there are multiple customer contacts, gatekeepers, and decision makers. Neither one is specific to the sales job you're going to be doing, but there are some very useful and relevant sections on the selling process, treated with a high degree of professionalism.

One thing I would always suggest is that you not leave yourself with only one option. If at all possible, set the stage for a decision point in which you have two or three viable job alternatives from which to choose. I know that's a lot more difficult (and time consuming and stressful) than you'd like, but it will result in a much better sense of "win" for you.

You're probably familiar with purchasing agents who refuse to deal with a sole supplier. They don't ever want to be in a position where a supplier can effectively hold them hostage. An employer who is actively seeking a new employee will similarly not hire the first person who walks through the door, even if the applicant meets all the criteria and would be perfectly acceptable. The employer wants alternatives, choices.

You should want some alternatives or choices for exactly the same reasons — so that you can't be held hostage. You owe it to yourself to have some options and to know what other possibilities are out there.

This takes real discipline, especially when you think you've found the perfect job and you could use a paycheck. The key is to try to bring a couple of prospective employers along at the same time, so that when it's time to make a decision, you have more than one option.

Moving into action

If you've tracked through this book to this point, you now have a philosophy, or a strategic perspective about what's about to happen in your life, and a limited set of "go do" next steps that will get you to your goal. You have a short list of books you'll want to get — either at the library, a local bookstore, or via one of the on-line booksellers.

Most importantly, you've now been given a framework or structure, based on traditional marketing thinking, that will help make this adventure a learning and growing experience instead of a nightmare.

For those of you who may be marketing students or practitioners, you'll recognize all the key elements of the traditional marketing mix in the chapters of this book. Of course, positioning has been identified explicitly because of its central role in marketing strategy, but I've dealt with distribution and sales issues, advertising, promotion and publicity, product, packaging, and pricing as well.

This book is not intended as a stand-alone, all-you'll-ever-need, how-to manual. There should definitely be other books on your list. The references I've specifically suggested have been reviewed and tested by time, and have proven effective in thousands of situations. Your job now is to trust the process and embark on your own journey.

Create the strategy and plans for the most important process you'll ever deal with. Not only will you learn a lot in going through the steps recommended here, but you'll be that much more valuable to yourself and your next employer because of what you've learned.

Good luck. I know that luck is an important ingredient in any project, but I also know that people who are well prepared invariably have better luck than those who are not. You have the strategic framework and tools at your disposal. Use them wisely and the luck will follow.

Appendix

A Brief Summary of the
Herrmann Brain Dominance Instrument
and Preferred Modes of Thinking

Let's start with a very rudimentary lesson about how the physical brain works.

If you're looking from the back of your head, the part of the brain nearest the scalp is called the neocortex, and this is the part of the brain where thinking occurs. Below that is the limbic part of the brain. That part deals with emotions and feelings. At the very bottom, at the base of the skull, just above your neck, is the reptilian portion of the brain. That's the part that comes into play when you're threatened and feel the need to either fight or run away. (This is frequently called the "fight or flight" response.)

Because it has three main components, this view of the brain is known as the "triune" brain. We're not going to spend any time on the reptilian brain, but we will use the neocortex and the limbic portions of the brain in this discussion.

Looking from ear to ear — left and right — we need to recognize that the two halves of the brain have different functions. The left side is associated with logic, order and structure, while the right side is more creative, free-flowing, and unstructured.

The two sides are connected by a very sophisticated communication system called the corpus callosum. The corpus callosum develops as we mature, starting larger and sooner in females than in males. This may explain why we tend to associate right-brain functions more with women than men.

What really happens is that ideas or thoughts that originate in the right side of the brain (usually in picture form) need to be expressed, and it's the left side of the brain that deals with language, communications, and organization. The ideas generated in the right brain travel over the corpus callosum so that the left brain can evaluate and express the ideas. (A great idea that's not communicated is like the tree that falls in the forest that no one hears; it's as though it never existed.)

Now, if we overlay the left-brain/right-brain understanding with the neocortex/limbic functions, we can visualize four quadrants of the brain:

♦ The *upper left/neocortex* (called the A quadrant by Herrmann) is logical and thinking. Scientists and mathematicians usually have real strengths in this area, as do many researchers and analysts.

♦ The *lower left/limbic* (called the B quadrant) is logical and more feeling. People who deal with processes, rules, and procedures generally have strengths in this area. This might include accountants, bookkeepers, administrative assistants, many lawyers, and people in the military, for example.

♦ The *lower right/limbic* (the C quadrant) is feeling and unstructured. These are people who can immediately become sentimental when they see a puppy or small child. They don't rationalize it; they just react naturally to visual cues. They often tend to be very people-sensitive and read body language quite well. Good HR and sales professionals often fit into this category, as do many artists and musicians.

♦ Finally, the ***upper right/neocortex*** (D quadrant) is thinking and less structured. These are big-picture folks, who tend to be holistic, intuitive, expansive, and creative in their thinking. They probably don't have a lot of patience for activities in the diagonally opposite B quadrant — detail oriented and process driven. They are often strategic planners, creative thinkers, and inventors.

It should be fairly obvious that most of us have multiple preferences. We think in different ways at the same time, though if we do have some strong preferences, we probably have less strong preferences for the diagonally opposite quadrant.

Now that you understand the basic structure of the metaphorical brain, you can probably imagine how a fairly straightforward self-assessment tool like the HBDI can map our thinking preferences based on responses to a series of carefully worded questions.

The "map" simply quantifies our tendency to prefer or avoid using each of the four quadrants of the brain when we are faced with a problem or decision. The quantification is on a scale that ranges from 0 to 133, so that you end up with four numbers — one for each of the quadrants — that, taken together, describe your profile. The profile, in turn, describes your preferred mode(s) of thinking — your natural tendency when solving problems or making decisions.

For convenience in discussing this in a "shorthand" way, Herrmann called any score below 34 "level three," or a thinking mode we tend to ***avoid;*** from 34 through 66 is "level two," or ***comfortable*** for use; 67 and above is "level one," or a ***preferred*** mode. (Anything over 100 is a "one-plus," or *really* preferred.)

To further facilitate communication, Herrmann and his staff frequently describe the profile by simply giving the level numbers in order, starting with A, then B, C, and D, so that you might be a "1-2-2-1," for example. That would mean you have strong preference (level 1) for using the A and D quadrants (the neocortex) and are comfortable (level 2) using the B and C quadrants (the limbic) when you make decisions.

Another profile — "2-1-1-1" — is the most common among women. It's a right-brain oriented profile, with an additional preference for the lower left (B quadrant) that deals with processes and procedures.

Male business executives tend to be left-brain oriented, often with an "avoid" score in the lower right — "1-1-3-2," for example.

Herrmann's research has shown that the most effective teams (a team is defined as two or more people working together toward a shared goal) have a collective "whole brain," or preferred mode of thinking (level 1) in all four quadrants. In small teams (like two or three people, for example) it's also important that there be at least one mode of thinking that is shared by the team members.

An example of this is found in the profile of two business partners I know. One has the profile 1-2-2-1, while the other has a 2-1-1-1 profile. Between them they have a preferred mode of thinking in all four quadrants, and they overlap in the D quadrant (holistic, big-picture, intuitive). The Herrmann approach would predict that they work very effectively as a team.

Another example comes from a married couple I know. His profile is 1-1-3-2 and hers is 2-2-1-1. They have all four quadrants covered (called "a whole brain"), but they don't have any area of overlap. He is left brained and she is right brained. They would probably be effective solving problems together, but they would come at it in such different ways that they might end up frustrated with the process.

Appendix: Preferred Modes of Thinking

The biggest problems occur when team members have level-1 thinking styles in diagonally opposite quadrants. Imagine a big-picture thinker (2-3-2-1, D quadrant preference) working closely with a team member who is into the details and standard operating procedures (2-1-2-3). They'd probably frustrate each other to the point where they couldn't really work together on a sustained basis.

Herrmann points out that you can often tell a person's thinking preference(s) by the language he or she uses. When presented with a new idea, someone with an A-quadrant preference might say "That makes good sense." A B-quadrant person might say "That's consistent with what has worked before." A C-quadrant person would say "That would be well accepted by everyone." And a D-quadrant person might say "That feels right," or "That fits the big picture."

They're all communicating the same idea (i.e., the idea is a good one), but they're saying it in the language that is consistent with their respective thinking styles.

By extension, it's a small step to profile an entire business team, or even a company, by combining the individual profiles of the members or leaders. It's usually pretty easy to spot telltale words in the chairman's comments on an annual report, for example. Similarly, a company's mission statement often contains signals that are important to understanding how management prefers to think.

The applications of the Herrmann approach are numerous, as you are undoubtedly beginning to understand.

Of course, this shorthand approach masks a lot of important detail, but it should help you grasp the basic idea and explain it to others in a way that will make some sense.

Remember that the HBDI measures thinking style preferences, not personality traits or behavioral tendencies. Don't fall into the trap of thinking that this one self-assessment tool can solve all problems. It's just a tool, and, like a hammer or a screwdriver, it has some applications in which it works just fine and others for which it is inappropriate.

The Herrmann Group has now administered the HBDI to more than 1.5 million people, and they've been diligent in tracking results, analyzing patterns, and drawing some tentative conclusions about them. Their findings, conclusions, and some interesting (and useful) extrapolations are well documented in the two books: *The Creative Brain* and *The Whole Brain Business Book*.

The description above is my own regurgitation of what I've read — not some kind of official dogma or sales pitch. It is intended to give you a general understanding of the underlying premise that forms the basis for Herrmann's work. If you're interested in this approach, I strongly recommend you find one of the books noted and see if I got it right.

There are, of course, other self-assessment tools, many of them quite good. I'm partial to the Herrmann approach for this purpose, though, because it's easy to understand and explain, and doesn't really require expert interpretation to be immediately useful. There are others that are more appropriate to specific applications, but they tend to be less straightforward, more complicated, and therefore not recommended for us amateurs.

Book List

In the course of reviewing the strategic elements of your plan to land the perfect job for you, I've mentioned several books and resources. If you're looking for a quick and easy synopsis of the key references, look no further. Here it is:

What Color Is Your Parachute?
By Richard Nelson Bolles

Since it was first released back in 1976, *What Color Is Your Parachute?* has become a "bible" for what Bolles used to call "career changers and job hoppers." The book is now reprinted each year and has grown to a 300-page encyclopedia of job search information, references, cartoons, witticisms, and philosophy. It's jam-packed with useful how-to information, quizzes, lists of search firms, and resources.

Sixth Sense
By Laurie Nadel, with Judy Haims and Robert Stempson

Grounded in scientific research, this book teaches you to trust your powers of intuition and make greater use of your whole brain. Interviews with the scientists who are exploring these new frontiers of the human mind, as well as celebrities who recognize and use the power of their own intuitive minds, make this a provocative and useful book.

Unfortunately, it's out of print in the United States right now, so you may have to settle for a copy at your local library. Alternatively, if you don't mind the British spelling and word usage differences, you can order a paperback version from Amazon.co.uk. It should cost about $15 to 20, including shipping.

The Evaluation Interview
By Richard A. Fear and Robert J. Chiron

When first published over thirty years ago, *The Evaluation Interview* gained immediate recognition as one of the best books on the subject of interviewing. Since then it has become widely acknowledged as an essential reference for organizations and personnel interviewers. It's not really "must" reading for the interviewee, but it could help to explain what's in the mind of a skilled evaluator as he or she assesses your suitability for a job.

The Creative Brain
By Ned Herrmann

The Creative Brain is a personal journey in discovering brain dominance. Ned Herrmann was a man with a mission — to help people understand their own mental makeup and know how to use it effectively. Herrmann had a twenty-year business career at General Electric as director of management education. He also enjoyed an active career as an artist — first as a singer and later as a painter. An illness forced him to abandon singing and take up painting, and his dual success as business leader and creative type led him to a study of the brain itself.

Moving from a physiological model, he devised a four-quadrant metaphorical model to define thinking styles that are measurable through a simple survey form — the Herrmann Brain Dominance Instrument. The book has enormous benefits for self-understanding, but goes beyond that to provide a means of dealing with others in the world of work and life.

The Whole-Brain Business Book
By Ned Herrmann

Most people and organizations, Ned Hermann noted, are stuck in a "brain rut" because their work is dominated by just one mode of thinking. Through practical explorations and exercises, he shows individuals and organizations how to harness the power of the whole brain. Readers can use *The Whole Brain Business Book* to expand their own thinking styles, to create and manage Whole Brain Teams, and to introduce new levels of flexibility and innovation into the corporate culture. It shows them how organizations like DuPont and GE use their "whole brain" orientation to thrive and profit in times of chaos.

The book is entirely business oriented. Key topics include thinking styles, management styles, communication, productivity, team formation, gender issues, creativity, strategic thinking, the thinking preferences of 773 CEO's from six countries, organizational change, "out of the box" thinking, entrepreneurship, reclaiming lost creativity, MBAs versus the creatives, managing financial crisis, and breaking down the barriers to whole brain growth.

Your Money or Your Life: Transforming Your Relationship With Money and Achieving Financial Independence
By Joe Dominguez and Vicki Robin

Your Money or Your Life is great reading for those seeking to reclaim their lives through financial freedom. Most readers will probably not follow the book's prescription in its entirety, but everyone will come away questioning their own priorities. The book has been around since 1992, and it's still one of the best guides to exploring your own relationship with money.

The 7 Habits of Highly Effective People: Powerful Lessons in Personal Change
By Stephen Covey

This book was a groundbreaker when it was first published in 1990, and it continues to be a business bestseller with more than 10 million copies sold.

Before you can adopt the seven habits, you'll need to accomplish what Covey calls a "paradigm shift" — a change in perception and interpretation of how the world works. Covey takes you through this change, which affects how you perceive and act regarding productivity, time management, positive thinking, developing your proactive muscles, and much more.

Grammar for Smart People
By Barry Tarshis

Based on the self-study program described by Forbes as "superb," this logically organized, easy-to-use guide is for anyone who wants to speak and write more effectively. It offers a readable and enjoyable reintroduction to grammar and usage in the English language. It teaches readers to distinguish between frequently used (and misused) words and phrases, and how to solve pronoun problems and learn the proper usage of verbs, punctuation, spelling, and more.

Grammar for Smart People is the title of both a book and a self-study course. You will need to contact the publisher — Salient, Inc. at (203) 454-5889 or on the Internet at http://www.salient-inc.com — if you want the original self-study program instead of the book.

"What Nerve!"

A brief interview with Michael A. Goodman

Interviewer: Given that you've been in the same job with the same consulting firm for the last 22 years, what makes you think you're qualified to give people advice about finding a job?

Goodman: Actually, I would submit I'm probably the *most* qualified person to deal with the subject. There are three reasons why I believe that:

First, consultants are ALWAYS looking for work. The moment I start a project, I'm thinking about the fact that the project is going to end, and I'll need another job. The average selling cycle in the kind of consulting I do is about a year, so I've already started my job search for next year.

I also know what it's like to have a hiatus in income, too much time on my hands, and the angst of not knowing what's coming next. It's part of the consulting lifestyle. So any job seeker who thinks he or she is the only person experiencing those traumatic emotions is sorely mistaken. Most consultants face similar challenges every day. I don't want any sympathy, but I hope you'll agree that maybe I've picked up some pointers about the job search process that can be helpful to others.

Second, the job search is fundamentally a marketing project, only most job seekers don't instinctively understand that. Either they don't understand marketing, or they don't recognize their challenge as a buying and selling situation. When you're a hammer, of course, every problem looks like a nail. And as a marketing consultant, the job search looks like a marketing project to me. When it's approached that way, the process works a lot better, is a lot less painful, and has a structure that is truly comforting in what can be the most stressful time of your life.

The third reason I feel qualified to discuss job search, though, is probably the most important: The research I did in preparation for writing *The Potato Chip Difference* uncovered some surprising truths about what works and what doesn't. Those are really the key nuggets of the book. Most job seekers, when they begin the job search process, are so eager to take action, to solve their immediate problem — to find a job NOW! — they actually do things that are counterproductive, obscure their real objectives, and sabotage their job searches!

It's not unlike the classical Hippocratic oath that physicians have pledged to uphold for centuries. The principle ethic of the oath is "first, do no harm." Before job seekers charge into the arena and do all the things they have to do in order to get a job, they first need to make sure they "do no harm." Only when they've done that are they ready to begin in earnest the implementation of a sound strategic plan for finding the job they want.

The things I've learned, and included in *The Potato Chip Difference,* are all the result of focused and concerted research in the area of job seeking and career planning. I've spoken with countless HR professionals, business executives, and job seekers in putting this together. I've read every book I could find on the subject, and on a whole host of related subjects. And I've been struck with the incredible parallels between a successful job search and a solid strategic marketing plan well implemented.

I don't know of anyone else anywhere who can make all these claims, and together they provide my rationale for why I'm the most qualified person to have written this book.

Readers are invited to visit the website

www.PotatoChipDifference.com

for additional information, publications,
references, and recommended
resources for job seekers.

The site also contains links to other helpful
websites and ordering information for all books
referenced in the **The Potato Chip Difference**.

Comments? You may contact the author

by mail:
c/o Dialogue Press
P.O. Box 657, Westport, CT 06881-0657

or by e-mail:
goodman@potatochipdifference.com

Personal Sense of Accomplishment Graph Notes

Age 0–7

Age 7–14

Age 14–21

Age 21–28

Age 28–35

Age 35–42

Age 42–49

Age 49–56

Age 56–63

Age 63–70

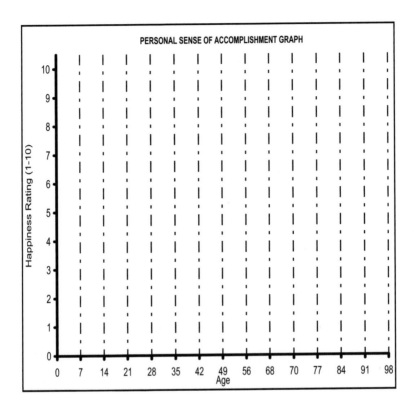

Age 70–77

Age 77–84

Age 84–91

Age 91–98

Core Values and Priorities

Personal Skills, Traits and Behaviors